LEADERSHIP TOUGH LOVE

EXAMINING LEADERS THROUGH THE LENS OF REALITY

Timothy Townley Lupfer

To Susan,
Great to meet you,
and I hope my insights
resonate in the great work
you do!

Tim

8 Dec 2024

INDIE BOOKS
INTERNATIONAL

ISBN-10: 1-947480-70-7
ISBN-13: 978-1-947480-70-4
Library of Congress Control Number: 2019911938

https://www.amazon.com/CicaSolution/b/ref=bl_dp_s_mw_8889597011?ie=UT-F8&node=8889597011&field-lbr_brands_browse-bin=CicaSolution&fbclid=IwAR2m19QaAn-8bO0HcoI_n_stJk2eOABVK2r84DKKHlVkZlNvzckiYw1pQCJM

Designed by Joni McPherson, mcphersongraphics.com

INDIE BOOKS INTERNATIONAL, LLC
2424 VISTA WAY, SUITE 316
OCEANSIDE, CA 92054
www.indiebooksintl.com

CONTENTS

PREFACE

I had just sat down to relax and catch up on magazine articles. I selected an article in a prominent business magazine with a cover story on leadership; the experience turned out to be anything but relaxing.

As I was reading, I wanted to let out a primordial scream. There, in this respected American business publication, was a list of today's top leaders. The article went so far as to call the list the world's *greatest* leaders. Of course, it contained the usual suspects—mostly high-ranking business executives and political figures. As I scanned the list, I wondered. Certainly, many of these high-level people were leaders in their current roles, because they were in positions of responsibility in large organizations with many employees. But just because they occupied the position, did this mean they were good leaders, let alone the world's *best*?

The article stated we can find leaders everywhere within organizations, but its list focused only on well-known people in high positions.

Are we so enamored with status that we assume people in high positions in large organizations are automatically the best leaders? It was sobering to recall that this publication (and many others) had lauded the disgraced CEOs of both Enron and Tyco as great leaders not too many years prior.

This list of the world's greatest leaders also contained sports stars and pop stars. But were those people really leaders? They are extremely talented *specialists*: people who possess extraordinary individual talents. Outstanding individual skill, however, does not automatically transfer into effective leadership, as the record in sports demonstrates. In this domain, the best individual performer frequently does *not* become a successful coach or manager.

The magazine went on to laud the list's sports stars and pop stars for their charity work. Without question, such efforts are worthy of praise. But had the stars in question simply lent their name to a cause and let others do the heavy lifting of leadership within the charity? There is nothing wrong with doing that for a good cause, but if this is the case, was this really an example of leadership of the highest order?

The inclusion of one pop star put me over the edge. I began to think, "Wait a minute. She's really only leading a small group of people—her entourage. She may be successful at affecting them to accomplish their common goals (and in that way, she may be an effective leader). Or she may be a *terrible* leader, turning over people like hamburgers at a fast food joint, succeeding only through the momentum of her individual talent and the revenue it produces. Yes, she has an amazing skill, and she is a celebrity. She has millions of people following her on Twitter. But that's not necessarily *leading*."

While I would hope that these celebrities really *are* effective leaders, I couldn't tell if they were or not. For one thing, this article didn't precisely define what leadership is, other than offering a timid list of seemingly unrelated attributes. As I pored over the so-called leaders named in this article, I began to realize that it was not really a list of leaders; it was merely a list of famous people—famous for occupying a particular position or having an outstanding individual talent.

The article reflected what I believe is a common error in our collective thinking today. We equate having broad *influence* with the ability to lead. Influence is one of the key tools for a leader, but other tools must also be in the leadership mix. We try to influence people all the time in all types of relationships: spouses, the boss, a volunteer group. That is not the same as leading, which is much narrower than the broader concept of influence. Leading occurs when you have designated followers—people whose actions you must affect to achieve the goals of the organization (the same organization that has designated *you* to lead those people). Leadership is a role, and not everyone performs in this specific role, including many famous people.

Leadership Tough Love: A Preview

The purpose of this book is to bring us back to what I believe leadership is:

Leadership is the role of affecting followers to achieve the organizational goals.

In discussing and applying this definition, I will introduce ideas and observations that will run counter to much current thinking on leadership, which is why I have titled my book *Leadership Tough Love.* Today I see too much sloppy thinking about leadership, too much happy talk, such as "everyone is a leader," or "real leaders don't need authority." To counter this, I propose we take a sober look at what leaders are and what they aspire to do. For us to identify, develop, and celebrate leadership, I wish to inject some tough love into the conversation. Each chapter in this book addresses a different, realistic way to look at leadership; each chapter contains blunt, even "heretical" thinking that runs counter to many of today's approaches. These thoughts may appear contrarian, but I believe they are a necessary corrective for current muddled thinking.

> **Leadership is the role of affecting followers to achieve the organizational goals.**

In the first chapter, I open with the harsh reality that hierarchy and authority are essential for leadership. I examine why leaders will always, by definition, operate within some form of hierarchy, even within the smallest group, because leadership is a distinct role, defined by whatever group we are in. From the family unit to huge organizations, we live within structures, or hierarchies. And we have hierarchies for two important reasons: first, without hierarchies, we cannot achieve anything on a large scale. We create hierarchical structures to direct our efforts and to manage our resources. Second, hierarchies, whether formally structured (organizational) or traditional (families and social groups), bestow authority, either formally or informally, designating who will lead.

Please note, leaders seldom emerge naturally from the group, due to the tyranny of time; hierarchy or structure are almost always involved in designating a leader's role. Authority should never be considered a dirty word; on the contrary, it is one of the essential tools of leadership.

Authority is the *complement* of the other key tool of the leader, influence. Successful leadership requires the effective exercise of *both* authority and influence. Neither tool should be relied upon exclusively over time by a leader, although in certain limited, short-term situations, either authority or influence could, and should, be used exclusively.

But despite organizational realities and challenges relating to leadership, there is also a significant organizational *limitation of scale* with respect to leadership: The most basic form of leadership, pure leadership, can only fully operate within smaller groups that have genuine relationships. This is a truly heretical thought. While organizations themselves can grow to larger scales, the range of an individual's pure leadership cannot expand beyond a limited number of followers under most circumstances. As humans, we simply cannot handle an increasing number of personal relationships beyond a certain point, so leadership in its most essential, basic form, *pure leadership,* is limited in scale to a smaller body of followers, as illustrated in the story of history's first consultant, Jethro, told in chapter 1.

In chapter 2, I present my definition of *leadership* (a very specific definition) and discuss the duality of authority and influence. My words may already raise red flags or generate complaints that I'm using out-of-date concepts like *authority* and *organization.* I beg to differ. These are not out-of-date concepts at all; rather, they are built into human behavior, and they will be with us as long as we operate in groups, trying to get people to achieve collective goals.

One of my observations of leaders throughout my life (including my own experiences as a leader) is that they can be extremely effective in one role, and then ineffective when they move to different roles. Chapter 3 explores the importance of the organizational context for any leader, suggesting that the "natural leader," effective in any and every situation, is a myth.

In creating leadership development programs during my career, I developed a leadership model that I believed defined the basic elements for effective leadership (direction, capabilities, and character) while also retaining the flexibility to fit into a variety of organizational contexts. In chapter 4, I examine these three basic elements and the importance of the organizational context.

I was pleased with this model until, during a presentation, I was presented with a challenge that shook my confidence in my entire approach. It was back to the drawing board with my leadership model, which I relate in chapter 5. The challenge: if leadership is so vital for organizational success, why are there so many bad leaders, especially at high levels? Even worse, why do so many bad leaders in high positions get away with it? I should have recognized from my own experience a very disturbing reality: that pure leadership is not scalable under most conditions, and that the higher one ascends in the organization, the easier it becomes to fake good leadership. This phenomenon is examined in chapter 6, Leadership Lite (which is effectively employing direction and capabilities as a leader, but lacking character).

My revised leadership model emerges in chapter 7. While my model, like any generalization, remains imperfect, I am confident it can help individuals who aspire to be leaders to be more effective and also help organizations develop their leaders more successfully, preparing capable leaders throughout the organization—especially at the highest levels (where, unfortunately, getting by with Leadership Lite is often easier). I also conclude with a taxonomy of leadership for organizations.

In chapter 8, I examine the difficult role of the executive with respect to leadership. I restate my view that someone in the highest organizational position (the executive) does not have to be the greatest leader in the organization, but must be a capable leader, and definitely must be an outstanding *manager*. Using lessons from recent acquisitions, I describe the danger of the *Executive Bubble*, a self-absorbed culture among some executives that breeds an unhealthy distance from the basic work of the organization and severely weakens leadership at the executive level by creating the *rent-seeking leader*.

One of the major themes throughout this book, supported by history and individual experience, is that tension is always present in all human relationships, including leadership. I use the expression *mere mortals* to describe nearly all of us as we aspire to overcome these natural tensions and lead effectively. But there is one rare exception: the charismatic leader—the leader who seems to be able to get followers to comply without friction. In chapter 9, I contend that this exception is rare and, when it does emerge, can be very dangerous.

We have all marveled at stories of heroic leadership. Thankfully, today we live in an era in which we seldom confront life-and-death struggles, so the demands for such exceptional leadership are very rare. Nonetheless, every leader needs to know how to recognize critical situations and how to step up to lead under those circumstances: the subject of chapter 10.

Has technology changed the context of leadership? Has the digital revolution expanded the capacity to lead on a greater scale? In chapter 11, "The Digital Delusion," I argue against that premise. I do suggest, however, that the recent increase in automation, driven by the ability to process massive amounts of data, is *reducing* opportunities to develop leaders in organizations, which is not a good trend.

Throughout this book, I emphasize that not all members of an organization should have leadership roles, and that this is natural and acceptable. I make the distinction between leaders (who must, to some degree, be generalists) and those who, in their roles, focus on detailed knowledge or on specific processes as individual pursuits. These are specialists. I predict that the increased complexity of our lives and coming increases in automation will create many more specialist roles than leadership roles in organizations. While I acknowledge that these two roles, leader and specialist, are not necessarily mutually exclusive, I do maintain that transitioning from specialist to leader becomes much more challenging throughout one's career, and that making a career specialist a leader late in his or her career is a very risky move. The distinction in roles between leader and specialist means that individuals should choose fairly early in their careers whether they want to take on the responsibilities of leadership. Not everyone who aspires to be a leader can be one; because of increased specialization, not everyone will even get the opportunity to lead.

Most importantly, many people actually wish to remain specialists and not assume leadership roles. Many specialists have made vital contributions to an organization's success, or to society at large, *without* being a leader. Specialists are as important for the success of collective endeavors as are leaders; however, I fear that we too often confuse these two very different roles, to the detriment of both.

How then, should individuals and organizations approach this narrower view of leadership and avoid confusing leadership with celebrity, merely occupying a position, or skill as a specialist? In chapter 12, I take on the persona of the Virtuous Machiavelli (addressing reality with the need for virtue) to offer ideas about leadership, the most important being the basic question: Are you eager to take on the burden of leading other people? If the answer is yes, always bear in mind a bitter truth: good intentions alone never deliver success. The impact of a leader's character, that vital element that is the source of good intentions, depends on a foundation of successfully giving direction and demonstrating your capabilities in your job. Competence counts, and that is acquired through practice in many different roles. Leadership's secret sauce (character) is only effective when it rests on the foundation of effective direction and capabilities.

While individuals must recognize that character without competence will not succeed, the dilemma that organizations face as they develop leaders is the reverse: *a leader's short-term individual success can mask deficiencies in character.* Clever, profoundly self-absorbed people can focus on key performance measures and either deliver them or fake them, irrespective of human damage along the way, and ascend to the top, eventually corroding leadership within the entire organization. In these conditions, cumulative improvement, the lifeblood of our society, can and will be sacrificed at the altar of excessive individual gain. As in so many of our endeavors, we can ruin things more quickly than we can build or repair them, and an organization's leadership culture is no exception. Once again, as the Virtuous Machiavelli, I offer my ideas in the final chapter, chapter 13, exploring how organizations should develop leaders to avoid this all-too-common disaster.

My Essays

All of my chapters are *essays* in the true sense of the word: *attempts*. I am attempting to save an essential role, leadership, from vague and mushy concepts, or from the cult of celebrity—errors that don't help mere mortals as we try to lead and, equally important, as we try to develop leaders. My essays don't provide neat and clean answers to every leadership problem, but I believe they will clarify important leadership concepts for use in the real world. To keep my ideas grounded, I employ real examples throughout this book, from history's wide sweep and from my own experience. I will not create cute caricatures to illustrate my thoughts, such as Suzy Psycho or Glad-handing Gary; rather, I will stick with the messy realities of what really happens or what really happened in history (at least, according to the accounts we have). I also refrain from overusing bullets and boxes as much as possible; I only employ plenty of bullets in the last two chapters when I discuss what steps individuals and organizations should take to develop leaders. My overall purpose in this book is descriptive, aiming to avoid a PowerPoint presentation under the guise of writing.

My goal is to wean us off the comfortable but erroneous beliefs that leadership is "natural" or easy, that people will follow a leader without any tension or resistance. In all my experiences in business and in the military, I have never seen anyone who achieved complete buy-in from every person he or she was leading. Even leaders with well-established reputations did not win over everyone all the time. Leaders face this challenge because followers have, or should have, some degree of autonomy. This autonomy is the greatest safeguard against tyranny, but this autonomy has only reached its fullest expression in our current, unique society, and the autonomy of followers will be constantly challenged by tyrants.

Learning From Dead White Guys?

I use several examples from history to illustrate many of my points about leadership. Most of these examples are taken from the history that I have known and taught: Western civilization. This naturally means most of the historical leadership examples are dead white guys. In our current culture, obsessed with identity, these examples may be controversial, but they should not be. My essays are infused with the idea of behavioral norms—universal, and independent of superficial labels. What can we learn from the dead white guys? As much as we can learn from *any* dead guy or gal, or any *living* gal or guy, of any origin. From both my experience with leaders and from the evidence of history, I fervently hold that leadership ability is completely independent of identity and labels. The trend in my lifetime is good: I am delighted that my granddaughters will have the same leadership opportunities as my grandsons.

Concepts such as Western society or Western civilization are under attack in certain circles today, but I would like to get beyond that to recognize that Western civilization is a unique development: a society that *aspires* to limit the use of force, through the rule of law, refined processes, and a culture of consensus. There is nothing hereditary or genetic about the benefits of Western civilization; these benefits belong to anyone who embraces these ideals and applies them, and I earnestly hope my audience is in that camp. These ideals have a profound effect on leadership because followers in the West have a significant element of choice which does not exist when raw power is the overriding factor in a leader/follower relationship. The exercise of raw power has been the norm for most of human history. Although aspects of power are present in any hierarchical relationship, the exercise of power (especially the use of direct physical force) is more restricted in Western society. This presents the Western leader with greater challenges than the leader who can automatically resort to force to gain compliance from his or her followers. But in the long run, the greater degree of autonomy of followers in the West also offers a vital advantage.

First, the challenges of this autonomy: Friction among free people is the rule, not the exception. Individual autonomy, or choice, creates tension in all human relationships, and the relationship between the leader and the led is no exception—just ask any parent of a two-year-old (the family unit is always the greatest laboratory for pure leadership). Therefore, we cannot expect immediate, unqualified, universal acceptance of any leader's actions; neither is unqualified acceptance of a leader a desired outcome (see chapter 9 on the dangers of charisma). Friction is a reality, and all leaders must learn to manage through friction to achieve organizational goals.

But keeping friction from becoming dysfunctional is not easy. One of the greatest leadership challenges today is when we must lead people to raise their standards of performance quickly and/or to change behavior significantly. This invariably invites resentment and resistance from followers, which many leaders are loath to face. We can see the results today in various institutions from education to politics, where positive trends are lacking because leadership cannot muster the courage to give a well-deserved bad grade or to address growing problems that exist beyond election cycles. Too much individual autonomy, unchecked by effective leadership, can make a group, society, or nation "unleadable" (which can lead to complete disaster, as I discuss in chapter 1).

But the good news is what effective leadership of autonomous (reasonably free) people can achieve: *cumulative improvement*. This is the vital ingredient that has improved the human condition more in the past 200 years than in the past 5,000 years of recorded history combined, let alone in the estimated 200,000 years that modern humans have been wandering on the planet. Cumulative improvement can be small and incremental, or it can be a dramatic, quantum change. What is crucial is the direction: a constant striving to make things better.

The Foundation Of Our Society: Cumulative Improvement

The hallmark of a culture of cumulative improvement is the ingrained drive to discover how to make things better. But this drive is a fragile, elusive force that is better nurtured than commanded. How does this relate to leadership?

Humans are not worker bees, those sterile creatures who genetically know their tasks and perform them obediently until they die. Yes, humans can be forced to perform, but in its most brutal form (slavery and other forms of bondage) force creates a culture of desperate survival, not improvement.[1] Even in a far less threatening form (the nasty boss at the office), a skewed, one-sided leader-to-led relationship will create a culture of *just getting by* for the follower. Cowering and keeping one's head down do not generate positive change, only resentful compliance. It is only where a member of a group can give his or her extra effort, that *voluntary,* discretionary effort on a sustained basis, that cumulative improvement can emerge, both in innovation and execution. Cumulative improvement does not occur solely by a mechanical decree from above, but through effective leadership that nurtures the discretionary effort at all levels.

In our endeavors today, organic forces (bottom-up ideas) must interact with mechanistic forces (top-down direction) in a careful balance, or sweet spot, so that cumulative improvement can be encouraged, achieved, and sustained. Leadership is critical at the so-called "lower levels" of the organization because that is where the insights for improvement often originate and is certainly where changes are almost always executed. Leadership is equally essential at the higher levels because that is where improvement is inspired, discovered, rewarded, and disseminated. The key word is *cumulative* because previous successes become the base for continuous betterment. Most crucially, this virtuous cycle cannot depend upon only one leader; to build something better, leaders must exist in *depth,* within the organizations and society, and in *breadth,* over time.

Within this desired cycle, the most outstanding leaders, *inspiring leaders,* leave an imprint—a lingering, positive inspiration that drives followers to strive for excellence, lasting well beyond the physical presence of that individual leader. In most cases, this imprint is formed over time through shared success, overcoming the inevitable friction that results when free people work together. Shared goals, mutual respect for each other's capabilities, and, most importantly, universal values that are reinforced by the leader's character are the elements that enable effective leadership. We desperately need this leadership today. We do not need

---

[1] Smith, Adam. *The Wealth of Nations.* Modern Library Edition. New York: Random House, 1937. See page 365: "A person who can acquire no property [a slave], can have no other interest but to eat as much, and to labour as little as possible. Whatever work he does beyond what is sufficient to purchase his own maintenance, can be squeezed out of him by violence only, and not by any interest of his own."

people who have achieved some form of notoriety or celebrity but who possess neither the skills nor character to lead.

Within our society today, we need leaders to restore our optimism through true cumulative improvement, not with smoke and mirrors or emotionally appealing slogans. We need leaders who can help us address and solve the long list of complex, difficult problems we face internally. Looking at the outside threats to our unique society, we need leaders to restore our resolve so we can protect our society and our cumulative accomplishments from the predators who would prefer that humans behave as worker bees to support only them. May my essays on leadership contribute to this purpose.

Timothy Townley Lupfer
Yorktown Heights, New York
January 2019

CHAPTER 1

In Praise Of Hierarchy?

THE PREVAILING POPULAR VIEW: *"We have a flat, nonhierarchical organization."*

TOUGH LOVE REALITY: *Impossible. Any endeavor of scale requires a hierarchy; we're stuck with it.*

The "Nonhierarchical" Illusion

In the 1990s, I had just joined one of the premier consulting firms in the world. As I entered this new and imposing organization, I had my antennae up to pick out common expressions in conversations with fellow consultants, because I have found that repeated expressions are good indicators of the real culture within any organization. I kept hearing a recurring theme: "We are nonhierarchical." This statement was made by several people, at all levels, and often. It was clear that by describing themselves as nonhierarchical, the members of this firm were laying down a marker, stating that their firm had a special quality. When I asked my fellow consultants how this quality manifested itself, I heard consistent responses that, within the firm, everyone's voice was heard with equal respect. In every internal meeting, input from any member was considered seriously.

Initially, my reaction to this supposed organizational quality was very positive. One of the underlying reasons given for this unique characteristic was that the firm engaged in a rigorous hiring process; many applied, but few were accepted. The talent was reputedly the best in the world.

Therefore, with such a distribution of outstanding talent, it made good sense that this firm would be a "band of brothers and sisters" where input and insights would be welcomed from all participants. Since the firm had demonstrated its wisdom by hiring *me*, how could I challenge such an admirable cultural attribute?

There was only one problem: This assertion of nonhierarchical functioning simply wasn't true in the real workings of the firm. First of all, the firm had a well-defined organizational structure, with ranks based on skills, experience, pay, and, above all, decision-making authority. It was nothing different from any other large firm. There was a clear career progression, and the rewards at the top were very enticing. The pyramid which one climbed to reach the top was also extremely steep, and the pyramid's slippery surface was lubricated by a ruthless up-or-out policy. Overall, it was an outstanding firm, but it was still a hierarchy.

As I engaged in my work with this firm, I began to observe the real organizational behaviors in meetings, especially in internal meetings that claimed to be nonhierarchical. As I observed team members reacting to input from colleagues, I saw what I had been seeing all my life in meetings (and at this point in my life I had already spent over twenty-five years in meeting-rich environments): instant deference to those in a position of greater authority. At the beginning of meetings, attendees introduced themselves, and each participant would then quietly gauge how important (within the firm) this or that participant was. Not surprisingly, the credence given to a participant's input was directly proportional to that participant's standing within the organization. Senior partners expected and received deference to whatever they said. The only exception I observed was when one partner formed a special group to focus on one important strategic theme. He made a genuine effort to solicit input from various sources, and he established a much more egalitarian approach. His experiment lasted less than two years, and then his group disbanded.

In my years with this firm, even though many aspects were outstanding, I began to grow weary of hearing the "We are nonhierarchical" mantra because I felt the statement was delusional. One day in utter frustration, after hearing that mantra once again, I shot back to that colleague, "No, this firm is more hierarchical than the United States Army!"

I was greeted with looks of horror. "Of course, you're joking?"

"No," I replied. "In the US Army, the hierarchy is obvious and accepted. It exists to clarify authority to make decisions. Hierarchy and input from below are not automatically mutually exclusive, and good leaders know that. In this firm, things are clearly just as hierarchical, but everyone runs around pretending it's not, and the flow up and down is simply not as healthy."

Human Beings: Wired For Status

While it may have been admirable for the firm to *aspire* to create a culture of less hierarchy, robotically stating the firm was nonhierarchical did not make it so. And I will now introduce the harsh reality about hierarchy: as much as we may claim to dislike it, hierarchy is inevitable if we want to operate at any significant scale.

We complain about hierarchy like we grouse about the weather; despite our constant complaints, it is always with us. And, ironically, we humans seem to adhere to hierarchy fairly well. Neuroscience studies suggest that we are alert to differences in status from a very early age.[2] We can even test this on ourselves; how many bosses do we remember vividly, versus subordinates, with the same level of clarity? Evidence indicates that we have a natural inclination to orient upward, toward the person with the higher status.

> The harsh reality about hierarchy: as much as we may claim to dislike it, hierarchy is inevitable if we want to operate at any significant scale.

Any organization that believes it can eliminate hierarchy is delusional. Hierarchy is the outgrowth of life's supply and demand. Our resources will always be limited because we

---

[2] Cialdini, Robert B. *Influence: The Psychology of Persuasion*. New York: Collins, 2007. See chapter 6 on Authority, pp. 206-236.

have a natural inclination to want more of almost everything. Especially with material things, there seems to be no limit to what we can aspire to consume. Since we do not live in an Eden of perfect abundance, we constantly have to decide how to divide limited resources (including the most vexing of resources, time). Therefore, decision-making authority will be structured within all groups, from small family units to large organizations. It is natural (and therefore inevitable) that members of any group will be keen to determine who possesses more decision-making authority within the group, and it is inevitable that people will devote more attention more often to those who possess that authority.

History's First Consultant: Jethro The Wise

Operating with complexity and increased scale reinforces the need for hierarchy, thus reinforcing our natural inclination to fixate on where someone fits within an organization. The inevitable nature of hierarchy was demonstrated more than 3,000 years ago in the account of the Jewish migration from Egypt to the promised land in the biblical book of *Exodus*, 18:13-27.

Moses and the Israelites had just entered Sinai, and Jethro (who was not an Israelite) came out of the mountains to visit his son-in-law, Moses. After exchanging pleasantries with Moses, Jethro observed how Moses was leading the Israelites. It was chaos.

Anyone could come directly to Moses with an appeal or question. Moses was consumed all day, every day, with these interactions.

The account states that Jethro said to Moses, "What you are doing is not good. You will surely wear out." Jethro then advised Moses to carefully select men of ability and the best character, and to establish a structure whereby small groups of ten Israelites would be led by a designated leader from this pool; these units would combine to form larger groups, led by other selected leaders, and this structure would build to encompass the entire body of Israelites. Only the most important issues would then be brought to Moses, at the top. Jethro said, "Then you will be able to endure. [These leaders] will bear the burden with you."

I love reading ancient accounts of human endeavors because I sense that our basic nature and many of the problems we face have not changed fundamentally over time. Jethro's advice was timeless and wonderfully wise: you can't manage everything; select people of ability and good character to deal with most of the issues; reserve the most important issues for your decision-making. Moses accepted his father-in-law's advice, and it worked. (Unfortunately for the future of consulting, there is no account of Jethro charging any fee for his advice.)

Relationships Versus Hierarchy: Dunbar's Number

But wait: Wasn't Jethro just an evil consultant who offered a bad solution? And, by the way, what *was* his fee? Wasn't he removing Moses from direct contact with his people?

No. Jethro was giving outstanding advice because we humans are limited in the number of relationships we can manage. Moses was simply incapable of managing every concern of every member of a large group, a constraint shared by all of us. The British anthropologist and psychologist, Professor Robin Dunbar, has developed a theory regarding the limit of the relationships we can manage by looking at primates and the size of their groups. By comparing the ratio of the volume of the brain's neocortex to the volume of the total brain, Dunbar uncovered a relationship between this ratio and the size (number of members) of the primate group. In the 1990s, Dunbar projected this ratio for the primate with the biggest neocortex of all, humans. The result was Dunbar's Number: the size of the social group one human can manage, which limits the number of people with whom any of us can have a direct relationship, while also knowing how these relationships interact. The actual number is a range between 100 and 200. Dunbar's Number is often expressed as the average, 150.[3]

This concept has been tested by examining hunter-gatherer societies, the least-developed and long-standing structures of human association (since current evidence suggests we have operated as hunter-gatherers for

---

[3] Konnikova, Maria. "The Limits of Friendship." *The New Yorker*, October 7, 2014. https://www.newyorker.com/science/maria-konnikova/social-media-affect-math-dunbar-number-friendships. Accessed May 27, 2019.

more than 200,000 years). As best we can gauge, the average number of members of these societies is around 150.

When I first learned of Dunbar's Number in the late 2000s, I was drawn to it immediately from my experience in the military. The fundamental unit in the land forces in armies today is the company, which is 100 to 150 soldiers. In any cohesive army structure throughout history, from the ancient Romans to the Mongols of Genghis Khan, this number has been maintained. This basic unit is commanded today in the United States by a captain; in ancient Rome, the unit was called a century, commanded by a centurion. Nearly all large military organizations have been built upon this basic unit.

Dunbar's Number immediately resonated with me because I had commanded both a company and a larger unit in the US Army (male-only in those days). When I commanded my company, roughly 100 soldiers, I knew every man. I knew his name, home state, and marital status. I knew where each soldier fit into the hierarchy. I also knew the basics of who was getting along with whom; the interaction of the relationships. Years later, when I commanded a tank battalion (composed of five companies), I tried to memorize the same information about each of my soldiers, as I had done when I commanded a company. The task proved impossible. I now commanded more than 550 soldiers, and my brain could not handle the data for a group that large. Much to my dismay, I could not maintain the same degree of relationships with all my soldiers as I had with the smaller company years before. That was the job of my subordinates, the company commanders.

The wise Jethro had anticipated Dunbar's Number three thousand years earlier. Relationships with our fellow humans can be wonderful, but we are limited by the mismatch between our brains and the size and complexity of our groups. Beyond a point, we cannot be all things to all people. To manage large groups—numbers of people beyond our capability for close relationships—we need structure. And with organizational structure comes distance between people and a heavy dose of standards, rules, and conformity. Is this structure more sterile and less intimate than the smaller group? Yes. This is a hard fact of our existence. It cannot be wished away.

The limitations of our relationships described by Dunbar's Number have, of course, been challenged, particularly in light of the digital revolution. In trying to keep up with the current research, however, I conclude that the number of digital "friends" one tries to maintain (with a genuine, not superficial, relationship) still falls within the limits of our brains. Hierarchy takes us beyond our basic relationships; if we are to operate in groups larger than our hunter-gatherer ancestors, we must embrace hierarchy, despite how much we may claim to dislike it.

This distinction (between the smaller group with deeper relationships and the larger organization with more remote relationships) has a tremendous impact on the nature of leadership in large organizations. Pure leadership, the leadership of close relationships, remains limited in scale. Close relationships between the leader and followers (immediate subordinates and staff) will exist at each level of the hierarchy, but they will not scale up to larger numbers. We must acknowledge and accept these limitations, because we can only accomplish large-scale goals through large, imperfect, and *impersonal* organizations.

Why We Need Hierarchy: The Failure Of Small Groups

We humans have always had a love-hate relationship with hierarchy, with the needle swinging back and forth. Our penchant for status leads us to work within a hierarchy, but we also shudder from hierarchy's control and impersonal nature. Our popular culture provides countless stories of how more democratic, egalitarian, and nonhierarchical rebels triumph over the evil forces of centralization and hierarchy. *Star Wars* is the most famous of this genre, and yet even that saga requires the constant reemergence of evil centralization to generate more villains (and more sequels).

Despite these emotionally satisfying popular stories, throughout history, hierarchy and its twin, greater centralization, have often overcome decentralized adversaries, especially when direct force was employed, irrespective of the virtue of one side or the other. In the United

States, most of our inhabitants today are descended, at least in part, from Europeans who arrived or invaded, depending on one's point of view. The land was already inhabited by people known today as American Indians, and these people were eliminated or pushed aside, first by disease, then by war, and finally by legal maneuvering. But while disease was the most devastating and one-sided factor (since indigenous peoples lacked resistance to European contagions), encounters in war were far less one-sided. From the first martial encounters, Europeans remarked on the bravery and endurance of the American Indian warriors they fought.

But these admirable qualities also pointed to a fatal flaw: the American Indians could seldom organize to achieve the scale needed to prevail in war against the invaders. In Texas, the Comanches were feared for their individual prowess and brutality in war; as one settler in an Old West story observed, if there had been 10,000 Comanches, they could have taken Washington, DC.[4] Such an event, of course, never came close to fruition. The Comanches could never coalesce into large fighting units.

Regarding the naming of the indigenous peoples of the Americas, there is still a lot of confusion and debate. I have used the term "American Indians" for two reasons: first, every person of American Indian descent that I have known would refer to him- or herself as a specific tribe first, and then use the term "American Indian" more generally. Surveys also indicate that this is the preferred term. Second, the United States Government uses the term "American Indian" in official titles, such as the National Museum of the American Indian. Irrespective of names changing over time, I have great respect for the original people who came to the Americas millennia ago.

Throughout the early history of the United States, American Indian tribes remained scattered and small, and they fought each other with equal vigor, often allying with European settlers to destroy rival tribes. In most encounters with settlers, the American Indian warriors displayed limited or no hierarchy. It was often difficult for the invading

---

[4] Foreman, Jonathan. "How Comanche Indians Butchered Babies and Roasted Enemies Alive." *Daily Mail Online*. Associated Newspapers, August 23, 2013. https://www.dailymail.co.uk/news/article-2396760/How-Comanche-Indians-butchered-babies-roasted-enemies-alive.html.

settlers to determine who was "in charge" as they dealt with their American Indian adversaries (which is also why the signing of treaties was frequently a farce).

One exception to this rule was the battle of the Little Bighorn, where the largest American Indian force, roughly 10,000 warriors, assembled, much to the chagrin of George Armstrong Custer and his soldiers. Custer is criticized in hindsight for splitting up his forces at the Little Bighorn, but this tactic had always worked for him before that fatal day, since the American Indians had never managed to put together such a large force before, nor would they ever again.

European settlers sweeping across North America were part of a larger European advance all over the globe, beginning in the late 1400s. The striking success of this advance is often attributed to superior technology, and that certainly was a key factor, but Europeans' *organizational ability* to operate at a superior scale was also decisive. Even the European advantage of superior technology diminished over time, especially in terms of weaponry. American Indian tribes adapted to muskets and rifles quickly, and the Plains tribes superbly adapted to the horse (which had been introduced to North America by the Spanish during the 1500s). American Indians seldom lacked bravery or skill in war, but they almost always lacked organizational scale. Ironically (and tragically), the American Indians needed more chiefs.

The failure of humans to organize in the face of disaster is not unique to any group, society, or culture. In the heart of Europe, the nation of Poland disappeared for over 100 years, primarily because its aristocracy would not unify and accept central decision-making to defend itself. From the late 1600s on, the Polish parliament (which was the gathering of the nobility, called the *Sejm*, often translated as the "Diet") became increasingly ineffective at governing, since any single member could veto any measure. The result was the lack of any capable central government. Throughout its history, Poland has never lacked rapacious neighbors; during the 1700s, Russia would play Polish nobles against each other and against whatever central government was trying to emerge in Poland, resulting in increasing paralysis and weakness in Poland. The final result was a complete dismemberment of Poland in 1795, with the territories of the former nation divided among Russia, Prussia, and Austria. The romantic appeal of Polish independence would arise frequently for the next 113 years, only to be brutally suppressed.

The harsh reality is that if we want to operate, or even survive, on a large scale, we must accept the trade-offs necessary to centralize, and that means we must grudgingly embrace hierarchy. We must sacrifice some individual autonomy, and we must accept weaker personal relationships to achieve anything in scale.

The Dark Side Of Hierarchy

Hierarchies will exist wherever two or more humans work together, even if this means a fluid trade-off in decision-making between partners—the most enduring example being the interaction between parents in the raising (and leading) of children. When we operate in smaller groups, where each person can establish a relationship with others, (operating within Dunbar's Number), we often have formal relationships overlaid upon informal relationships, a dual-track system for getting things done. When these two tracks reinforce each other, it is a joy to work within the group. When conflict or contradiction emerges between these two tracks, the small group becomes dysfunctional.

But when we organize in numbers beyond Dunbar's Number (and we must if we are to achieve anything of scale), hierarchy and its formal structure become more important and frequently override informal relationships. Close relationships still exist, but they are confined to the smaller groups within the larger structure. *When organizational scale increases, people really do become numbers.* The development of hierarchy to manage at scale is not inherently evil, since it is merely an acknowledgment of the limitations of our abilities to manage close relationships on a large scale. But operating at a scale beyond personal relationships can certainly lead to disastrous consequences on a large scale, especially when leaders in high positions lack direction, capability, and, most importantly, character (the three key elements of leadership, to be discussed in detail in chapter 4).

One of the dark accompaniments of hierarchy is effective coercion. The use of force can be observed in any human organization irrespective of size, but large-scale hierarchy can exhibit coercion on steroids since centralization can effectively amplify force. Numerous experiments have shown that we treat each other better when we have some sort of mutual relationship with the other party; when the other party is just a number or considered to be different from us, we tend to behave more harshly toward him or her. For example, even in experiments where solely artificial differences are created between groups, we treat members of the "other" group worse than we treat members of our own group.[5] Throughout our 5,000 years of recorded history, there has been a direct link between the size of the state and its ability to monopolize, enhance, and employ force, both on its outside adversaries and on its own citizens. As the quotation attributed to Josef Stalin, who certainly delighted in using force on a massive scale, illustrates, "A single death is a tragedy; a million deaths is a statistic."

If the reader of this book lives in the West, he or she enjoys the rare condition in which the use or threat of physical force by the state (or by any large organization) is significantly constrained, by both laws and culture. But I also use the word "coercion" to mean compulsion other than by physical force. Compulsion is any action taken by the organization to enforce compliance employing any tool beyond persuasion. This leads to the second harsh reality about hierarchy: All hierarchies contain within themselves some potential degree of coercion. As Yale Law Professor Stephen L. Carter has observed to his incoming law students, "...every time we enact a new law, we create the possibility that violent means will be required to transform the new law's command into reality."[6] The laws and societal norms that restrict the use of force within our societies in the West are precious, fragile, and very rare in the course of human endeavor. But while the use of force within hierarchies is constrained in our societies, it is certainly not absent.

---

[5] Whitbourne, Susan Krauss. "In-Groups, Out-Groups, and the Psychology of Crowds." *Psychology Today*. Sussex Publishers, December 10, 2010. https://www.psychologytoday.com/us/blog/fulfillment-any-age/201012/in-groups-out-groups-and-the-psychology-crowds.

[6] Carter, Stephen L. *Civility: Manners, Morals, and the Etiquette of Democracy*. New York: Harper Perennial, 1999.

"You're fired!" is an act of coercion in an organization, because it states that the organization no longer will tolerate the person's membership within the organization; that person has no input in the decision and often has no chance to appeal. Therefore, some form of coercion will always be present in any hierarchy, from the authority to assign work to the power of performance reviews, to (finally) the termination of the work relationship. The effective leader knows which potentially coercive tools he or she can use and when to use them, because the answer to the desperate cry, "Why can't we all just get along?" is that, regrettably, we simply cannot. Authority conveys organizational power to the leader, and it will always be a vital tool.

Can this tool of authority be abused? Certainly. It is abused all the time. With centralization, the easy default for leaders at the top is to rely on concentrated authority and force, and that has been the pattern for most of our history. But we in the West live in a very fortunate era when the use of coercive power is limited. Our incredible abundance (unprecedented in human history) and free-market economy mean that most people are not driven to utter desperation with a bad turn of events, such as being fired. In the West, we may fear "You're fired," but in many other parts of the world, the command "Fire!" is employed instead, with far more lethal consequences.

Leaders and Hierarchy: Final Thoughts

Being "nonhierarchical" is a myth. Not only will some degree of structure for decision-making always exist in any endeavor, but the structure itself also communicates the primary message about who is a leader, and therefore, who possesses authority over others.

When an organization designates us as a leader, we should not deceive ourselves about whether we would be the "natural" choice of the followers. That consideration is a waste of time because the overwhelming number of leadership roles we will occupy will be assigned by an organization or a societal event (for example, becoming a parent). What matters is that we have been given the responsibility to lead. Now we need to consider how to be effective in that role, and how to overcome the inevitable friction that exists among autonomous people, by earning the trust of those we lead.

CHAPTER 2

OK, So What *Is* Leadership?

THE PREVAILING POPULAR VIEWS:
"Everyone in our organization is a leader."
"Real leaders don't need authority."

TOUGH LOVE REALITIES: Not only is everyone in an organization not a leader, several people don't want to be leaders, and that's OK. Authority is a valid tool that leaders must know how to use.

I n the early 1980s, I was stationed at Supreme Headquarters Allied Powers Europe (SHAPE) in Belgium, the military arm of NATO. One afternoon, a small group of midlevel officers (majors and lieutenant colonels) got together in an office during a bit of down time to have a bit of fun. One of the officers (from the United Kingdom, as I recall) was a very good cartoonist, and with group input, he prepared a series of cartoons about officers from each of the NATO countries, funny depictions of the "ideal" NATO officer modeled on stereotypes drawn from each nation. Yes, it was a bit politically incorrect, but it was funny, as well as a useful window to show how people from other nations saw each other.

As we all went over the cartoons, we had some good laughs. The ideal NATO officer is "as straightforward as a Brit," with a cartoon of a British officer putting a knife in the back of another. "As well-organized as an

Italian," "As generous as a Netherlander," "As humorous as a German," and so on. (The Germans in our group did not think their stereotype was very funny.) As this was proceeding, the Americans in the group began to wonder how we would be portrayed. The United States was the largest force in NATO and always an inviting target, so how would we be skewered? The artist then came to our cartoon: "As flexible as an American," with a drawing of a US Colonel pointing to a book of regulations. The Americans in the group were shocked. "We're not like that," we shouted. Every non-American officer looked at us and said, "Oh yes, you are."

The shock to the Americans was generated because we Americans don't picture ourselves as being inflexible. Aren't we practical about how we get things done? But the important lesson I learned that day is that your own self-image may be very different from how others see you. From that day forward, I began to step back from the various attributes we ascribe to ourselves, to determine a bit more objectively how we might really be behaving, both collectively (in terms of American culture) and individually. I began to observe that we Americans actually *are* very process-oriented, to the point of appearing rigid (and I have observed this in business as well as in the military). We like to follow rules and prescribed steps, and overall that's a good thing, even though this came across as inflexibility to my fellow NATO officers. I often reminded my non-American military friends (to reinforce our American process-orientation) that we American officers had sworn to defend our Constitution, which is not only our laws, but also our process for government, while many of the European officers had declared allegiance to a monarch. We Americans must love process—we have the largest number of lawyers, per capita, of any nation on earth.

Because I've worked throughout my life with people from several different countries, particularly from Europe, I have been able to discern a few more peculiarities about Americans. One national characteristic I would love to reverse is a tendency to be sloppy about definitions. Countless times I have seen Americans jump in to solve a problem, flinging high-sounding terms around, without clarifying what those terms are supposed to mean. We Americans often lack precision in the words we use; our politicians are the worst offenders. I have contrasted that behavior to that of other nationalities, whom I have often observed taking great pains to lay out definitions in advance of a discussion. That effort might seem a bit tedious at first, but I have observed that such clarity is very useful in the long run.

We all throw out the word *leadership* constantly, but I want to define this term, and my definition is probably narrower and more nuanced than the concepts many Americans may have in their heads as they discuss leadership:

Leadership is the role of affecting followers to achieve organizational goals.

First, this definition assumes a hierarchy, an organization, in which the leader is operating. I offer this critical assumption because I maintain that most of us who are leading, most of the time, are doing so within an organization that has some structure for decision-making, either formal or informal. We are probably most familiar with the image of the large organization, but leadership relationships are also established by culture and tradition, such as within the family. Parents are the leaders of their children, both by custom and by biology (humans are hopelessly helpless at birth and require the longest period of any animal to develop independence).

Here I must also introduce another contrarian thought: the maxim that "everyone [in a given organization] is a leader" is nonsense. Many people fulfill important organizational roles who want *no part* of leading. Many people are quite content to operate as an individual specialist, having no direct responsibility to get other people to do anything. True, it can be confusing when a specialist is called a "leader in her or his field," but this use of the word "leader" means an outstanding individual performance, not the assuming of a role to get followers to achieve a goal.

The purpose of leadership is also made clear in this definition: It is to achieve *organizational* goals. Although I maintain that the *art* of leadership in its purest form is intensely personal, its goals should never be *exclusively* the personal goals of the leader. To use a favorite business buzzword, the goals of the leaders and the goals of the organization should be aligned. But to be clearer, I believe organizational goals should be the overriding standard, and the personal goals of the leader and followers should conform to them. This implies a degree of shared interest in achieving the goals, not just between the leader and the organization, but also between the leader and the followers—a crucial element in preventing an entirely one-sided relationship between leaders and followers which, in its worst and most extreme form, is tyranny. This crucial alignment reinforces one of the basic assumptions of my approach to leadership—this critical interaction between leaders and followers assumes that followers have some degree of choice because they are independently thinking human beings.

Autonomy And The Discretionary Effort

The existence of choice among followers in our free society, even in subtle forms, became very striking to me immediately as I began my career in the US military. Outside observers to military culture often think, "People are compelled by law to obey, so you just have to give a bunch of orders and they will comply." In reality, any second lieutenant finds out in about ten minutes that soldiers can demonstrate amazing discretion in how they comply.

For example, subordinates can do the minimum of what is required, performing exactly what was asked, and no more. Or at the more positive end of the spectrum of behavior, they can, in good faith, address the spirit of what was directed by the leader, and then apply their own judgment to refine their performance further and produce a better outcome. This second form of response reveals the key component of outstanding leadership: obtaining the *discretionary effort* of the follower. At Ft. Carson, Colorado in the 1970s, a fellow company commander once described what this discretionary effort can mean. We were discussing our new big boss, Colonel Y, the new brigade commander, and comparing him to his predecessor, Colonel X. My colleague put it this way: "If we were at war and Colonel X were taken prisoner, I would personally lead the effort to rescue him. If Colonel Y were captured, I'd send someone else to lead the rescue effort."

Fortunately for the newly arrived Colonel Y, his subordinate's degree of discretionary effort was never tested in war.

The First Indicator That You're A Leader? The Organization Says So

What is the first way people in an organization know the status of leaders and followers? Most often, the organization designates it. Since we humans are very sensitive to status, we pick up on these designations very quickly. And let us not be fooled by "nonhierarchical" talk and grand gestures, such as open floor plans—we all quickly figure out who makes the most important decisions, and we adjust to that status.

As Moses learned from Jethro, hierarchy is a practical means (structure) to achieve an end (a better use of talent to make decisions). Hierarchies become distorted and less effective when they are seen as an end in themselves—when achieving the position and enjoying the status of leadership becomes the end game, instead of achieving organizational goals through effective decision-making. Both leaders and followers can contribute to this distortion: leaders, by seeking only the perks of the position, and followers, by attributing excessive, unrealistic powers to leaders (and thereby also denying *their own* responsibilities).

Authority is a powerful tool, and even in the relatively democratic West, authority is most often bestowed by the organization. To be effective leaders and to develop effective leaders, we must accept the use of authority as a proper tool for leadership and stop pretending that authority is outmoded or unimportant. We must resist the delusion that, in our interactions in an organization, things will simply flow naturally, and we'll all work for a common goal without friction. There is friction in all human relationships. We can work through it, but we will never eliminate it. Structure and defined authority are useful approaches to give clarity and to reduce friction, when used with care.

How Does The Leader Affect Followers? The Duality of Authority And Influence

To explore the definition of *leadership* further, we must examine how leaders affect their followers to achieve organizational goals. I submit there are two basic tools for a leader to employ: authority and influence. As described above, authority is formal and bestowed by the organization. In contrast, influence is informal and generated by the leader him- or herself. Ideally, these two forces mutually reinforce each other in the behavior of an effective leader. The effective use of these two instruments is the key duality of leadership: the skillful balance of these two basic tools. This authority/influence duality mirrors the larger organizational duality of mechanistic direction (top-down) and organic emergence (bottom-up), to be discussed in detail in chapter 3.

Authority, like *hierarchy*, is a word that many people today acknowledge only with great reluctance. But authority, a product of hierarchy, is a fact of organizational life. Possessing authority is the primary signal of a leader's status, the organizational shorthand for designating who will lead whom. Most leaders, most of the time, are assigned to their positions through some process within the organization, and rarely does this entail any democratic process involving the followers. Just as some people try to wish away the existence of hierarchy, so will some people pretend that authority isn't necessary, that it is a crude club wielded when persuasion would be much more effective. That gross generalization is delusional happy talk. As historical examples show, from constant internecine squabbling among American Indians facing an existential threat to the dithering of the Polish Diet, we don't have the luxury of time to keep everyone happily engaged all the time. We have to make decisions with limited time and imperfect knowledge. Friction will never be too far from the surface. To bring along reluctant followers, especially if time is limited, the instrument of authority, bestowed by a hierarchy (or by other means, such as biological necessity in the case of parents), is essential.

Authority is the formal force behind a leader's decisions. But authority is strong medicine—the key to its effectiveness is dosage. And like effective medicine, authority is often abused (or overprescribed) precisely because it is so effective.

Know How To Use The Medicine

Because we naturally incline toward those in power, authority is a powerful tool for a leader. Therefore, it behooves a newly appointed leader to understand the scope and limits of his or her authority when assuming a leadership role. I have seen errors by newly appointed leaders at both ends of the spectrum: new leaders who rely too much on authority, and newly appointed leaders who begin on the wrong foot when they think the magic of their own personality will bring everyone together, only to face resistance and not know how to address it.

All forms of authority encompass some degree of coercive power, even if this is subtle or unacknowledged. As previously discussed, one of the great accomplishments of Western society is the attenuation of physical force through defined processes, but some residual coercive power remains in all organizations, even if it is merely the ability to evaluate performance. Leaders need to know what formal tools of authority they possess to address any friction that could impede progress toward organizational goals, ranging from insubordination, to lack of cooperation, to poor performance, or to subtle resistance. Leaders need to understand the nature of their authority *before* they face these inevitable challenges. This knowledge of authority, as well as its range within the leader's position and how to use it, is fundamental for leadership success. For example, every successful executive with whom I have worked, without exception, knew how to employ his or her authority, including bringing the hammer down when the situation required it.

But formal authority should never be the *sole* instrument leaders employ to affect their followers. Unfortunately, because of our inherent deference to power, the use of authority to affect followers can become the lazy default for poor leaders. This crude approach—excessive reliance on authority—will only yield *compliance*, which may suffice in the short run, but will not inspire the enduring, discretionary effort that organizations need to improve. For this, the complement of authority is essential: influence.

The Other Instrument: Influence

Influence is defined as leadership aspects that emerge from the behavior of the leader him- or herself: aspects that are not based on the formal authority of position. This leadership tool is much more complex and diverse than authority, both in the range of behaviors and in their degree of impact. Whereas I have observed that successful executives always know how to employ authority, I have found the record much more mixed with regard to the effectiveness of influence, probably because it was more varied and indirect in its impact on followers.

Influence offers a wide range of behaviors, some tied directly to the leader's performance, while other instruments remain more subtle. One key difference between influence and authority is the factor of time: Authority is bestowed immediately by the position, derived from the authority of the organization; influence requires an investment of time to be effective with followers. Ironically, constant personnel churn in an organization, whereby people move rapidly from one role to another, frequently diminishes the effect of leader influence and makes leaders more dependent on authority.

To survey the behaviors that leaders can use to influence their followers, I employ three basic categories of influence: unconscious influence, direct interactions, and reputation. Picture a leader you have known and consider how, apart from authority, this leader affected you through these categories of influence. Perhaps the most vexing of these categories is the first: unconscious influence (sometimes the term "nonconscious" is used). It is beyond the scope of this book to address unconscious influence, a subject of considerable complexity, in full detail. The most important lesson for a leader to understand is that we humans are influenced by events that we absorb subliminally, that is, below the level of our consciousness. This insight is relatively new. We gained it within the last 100 years; before that, received wisdom told us our behaviors were all conscious actions. Sigmund Freud was one of the first to popularize the role of the unconscious in shaping our behavior, and unlike many of his other theories, this one has been shown over time to be accurate, especially based on recent studies employing functional MRIs of the brain. The insight about the role of the unconscious is that we humans send and receive signals to each other of which *neither party is consciously aware*; this applies to leaders as well as followers.

For example, can unconscious factors such as good appearance and being taller positively influence followers, at least initially? In general, yes. These and several other subliminal factors can assist the leader in influencing his or her followers, and leaders should be aware of these subtle influences. Accordingly, leaders should grasp the importance of appearance and its ability to affect subtle communication, especially when meeting people for the first time. I have seen leaders (and I certainly have been guilty of this error myself) appear disorganized and disheveled on first meeting subordinates. In one case I observed, a newly appointed leader appeared at an initial meeting with his new team in a rushed state and came across as being completely unprepared. Over the next two years, this leader never recovered from this error, having lost the respect of his group at the outset. While most of us are not born with movie-star looks, above-average height, or a body that makes fat melt away, we can at least make an effort to present ourselves in the best light possible, knowing that we are all constantly communicating just below the surface of our collective consciousness. A way to test this is to ask yourself: Do I prepare as carefully for the first meeting with my subordinates as I do for my first meeting with my boss?

To improve our influence with our followers, we have much more control over the second influence, our direct interactions, and here we can also benefit from findings from neuroscience. For example, in communication, leaders should recall that we humans are predominantly visual. The much-repeated concept of learning styles of visual, hearing, and tactile is not supported by evidence; a recent article in *The Economist* labeled this concept "pseudoscience" and "nonsense."[7] In terms of the

---

[7] Together, Technology and Teachers Can Revamp Schools." *The Economist*, July 22, 2017. https://www.economist.com/leaders/2017/07/22/together-technology-and-teachers-can-revamp-schools.

neurons in our brains, we devote more effort to processing visual input than to all the other senses combined.[8] We also expend a lot of brain energy in such visual actions as face recognition. Leaders should capitalize on these tendencies: Conduct face-to-face meetings when possible, use visual contact (digital meetings) before phone calls, and make phone calls before emails. Although our digital world keeps advancing the idea that we can successfully operate remotely, I suggest we stick to what has facilitated our interactions for over 200,000 years and try to meet face-to-face as much as possible.

Influence Requires Time

Influence skills must be developed and honed over time, through practice and trial and error. The context in which we operate is also often in flux—our audience (our body of followers) can change, so we must constantly monitor the context in which we are delivering our communications and adjust accordingly. While we need to be especially careful about how we conduct our first encounters with key people, we must also recognize that positive influence requires time to be effective. Very few of us can completely engage people immediately, to employ irresistible influence over others upon the first meeting. Irresistibility, or charisma, is very rare; it is too often confused with the effects of reputation (far more common). Furthermore, in most instances in history, charismatic leaders have been dangerously destructive (as I relate in chapter 9).

The third category of influence is most dependent on time: reputation. This is the leader's traveling narrative: the set of stories reflecting the leader's effectiveness. Please note, again, the precise nature of this definition. *Stories* is the key word because the human interpretation of the leader's actions through stories constitutes reputation. A leader can certainly be measured on performance, but the numbers themselves usually do not tell the entire story; it is the human assessment—how he or she accomplished something—that becomes the core of the reputation.

---

[8] Grady, Denise. "The Vision Thing: Mainly in The Brain." *Discover* magazine, June 1, 1993. Of the neurons in the cortex, processing vision takes up 30 percent, while 8 percent process touch and 3 percent process hearing.

Especially as one ascends the ladder of an organization, stories begin to follow the leader, and will often precede the leader as he or she attains a new position. These stories can take on a life of their own. When I was a captain in the US Army and commanding a tank company (100 soldiers) in the mid-1970s, I was obsessed with keeping a high maintenance record for my vehicles. Our tanks were out-of-date models with constant maintenance problems, but I was determined to get as many running as possible. One story that circulated about me was that I had tied string from the tank commanders to the drivers in my tanks so that the tank commander (in the turret) could signal the driver (in the front of the tank) to turn left, right, or halt. The story was that this rigged system still satisfied the safety rule of constant communication between the tank commander and driver, even if the tank's intercom (the actual *designated* means of communication between the two) was not functioning. In other words, I kept a tank running by jury-rigging it with string to enable communication. This story was utterly false; I never took such a careless risk because I was equally obsessed with safety—the intercoms had to work to move the tanks. But the story of "that crazy captain who did anything to get the tanks rolling" became part of my reputation.

Reputation is the informal report card on how a leader is perceived by followers, and it shows how the larger organizational context can affect a leader's efficacy. Reputations can be accurate or inaccurate, fair or unfair. Reputation is also the way a specialist can exercise an indirect form of leadership. This is often the only form of leadership a specialist wants to exercise, and indirect leadership may be the only form of leadership that a specialist *can* exercise. In the domain of sports, Babe Ruth desperately wanted to become a baseball manager after his playing career was over, but his reputation for out-of-control behavior hurt him. One baseball executive said, "How can he manage other men when he can't even manage himself?" and this was probably the attitude of many others in baseball.[9] The Wikipedia entry for Babe Ruth confirms that his failure to

---

[9] The baseball executive was Ed Barrow, the director (a position that is now called general manager) of the New York Yankees in Ruth's era. The quote is taken from Corcoran, Cliff, "99 Cool Facts about Babe Ruth," *Sports Illustrated*, posted July 14, 2013.

gain a job as a big-league manager was "most likely due to poor behavior during parts of his playing career." Being the greatest player of his era (specialist) did not guarantee an opportunity to *lead*. Individual skill and leadership ability are very different.

The ground beneath the leader's feet will always shake from the movements of the organization itself and of society at large. Forces that move within our organizations come not only from the top down; they also evolve from the bottom up. In a rush to just get things done, we often overlook the organic, or bottom-up forces, and we forget that understanding these forces is crucial to our leadership success—the subject of the next chapter.

CHAPTER 3

The Bigger Context: Organizational Dynamics

THE PREVAILING POPULAR VIEW: *"Change and innovation are most often directed from above."*

TOUGH LOVE REALITY: *Change, and especially innovation, are a delicate combination of mechanistic (top-down) and organic (bottom-up) forces, with the organic forces playing the bigger role in most cases.*

W e all seem to be wired to focus on status. That inclination drives us to concentrate on the decisions made by those above us. In effect, we are psychological prisoners of hierarchy. That is why, for most of us, history is seen as a direct cause-and-effect link between decisions from above and outcomes. This tendency is reinforced by the fact that scribes, working for those who made such decisions, have done most of the history writing over the millennia. Only in the past few hundred years have Western historians tried to shift the focus, to examine what forces in history have evolved from the bottom up, as opposed to coming from the top down. This approach is laudable, but it will always encounter some skepticism, even subconscious resistance, since this approach cuts against the grain of our natural focus on decisions at the top.

My *aha* moment recognizing the power of forces from the ground up occurred as I prepared for a family trip to China in 1988. Since I didn't know much about Chinese history (and since I wanted to get the most out of this trip), I went through several books in the library, and one theme seemed to dominate: Chinese historians tended not to view their history as a linear progression, but as a cycle. Their history was viewed, not as a relatively straight line sloping upward (the Western view of its own history from 1500), but as a sine wave repeating the nation's ups and downs as cycles every few hundred years. The cycles in Chinese history occur in a pattern: a new dynasty is established and begins to rule wisely; the nation is prosperous. Over time, the dynasty becomes corrupted, and the condition of the people deteriorates. Finally, someone rises up from among the people, overthrows the ruling dynasty, and establishes a new dynasty. The cycle begins again. A useful way to describe these forces, in English, is to call the top-down actions of the dynasty *mechanistic* and to call the forces that rose up against it *organic*.

An American Case Study: The GI Bill

Using this framework of these two forces, mechanistic (top-down) and organic (bottom up), I began to look at various historical events differently. I tried to overcome my natural inclination to fixate on top-down decisions, and instead examine what forces were brewing at the base, that working end at the bottom of the hierarchy, both in society at large and in organizations. What I began to discover was that many successful outcomes depended very much on organic, or bottom-up, actions. My favorite example is the Servicemen's Readjustment Act of 1944, better known as the GI Bill. The greatest outcome of this legislation was raising the overall level of education of the United States workforce during the postwar era, thus significantly improving the human capital of the country in one generation. My father, a US Navy aviator in World War II, was one of the millions who benefited from this enlightened legislation.

But then I discovered that this impressive outcome was not the purpose of the bill; the actual purpose was much narrower. After the *first* World War, the United States had suffered a brief but severe depression in 1920-21 (often labeled the Forgotten Depression, thanks to the bigger one that began in 1929). One of the causes of the Forgotten Depression was the inability of the country to absorb returning veterans into the workforce. Learning from the problems of the immediate post-World-War-I difficulties, the framers of the GI Bill in 1944, anticipating the coming end of World War II, developed a more comprehensive approach for soon-to-be-returning veterans. Their scope was broad, including mortgage assistance, veterans' hospitals, and tuition assistance for college and training. One of the perceived advantages of offering tuition assistance was to keep huge numbers of veterans from immediately entering the workforce, thereby avoiding the problems the country experienced after World War I. Therefore, the mechanistic, or top-down, direction for the GI Bill was practical and targeted: Let us offer this menu of benefits to our veterans, and let's soften the impact of this huge number of returning veterans (about fifteen million, more than three times the number of returning World War I veterans) by encouraging them to go to school before they re-enter the workforce.

The Power Of Organic Forces

The somewhat limited scope of the GI Bill was met with a tremendous response from below, from the millions of veterans themselves. The actual enrollment of veterans for education and training during the postwar era far exceeded initial estimates. Nearly nine million World War II veterans attended some form of education or training under the new GI Bill. Many educational institutions were overwhelmed with the numbers, but at the grassroots level, the problems were overcome. Millions of families, including my own, heard stories from their World War II veterans about college lectures being broadcast in hallways to accommodate the huge numbers of students, and about problems finding places to live on or near university campuses. But at the organic level, determination to make this program work overcame these obstacles.

Recipients embracing the GI Bill's education and training opportunities created long-term benefits for the nation that were most likely not part of its original intent. American colleges and universities granted twice the normal number of degrees in the immediate postwar period. "Going to college" became far more common in the United

States, a trend that continues today. Before World War II, fewer than 5 percent of Americans earned bachelor's or advanced degrees. By the year 2000, nearly 25 percent of Americans had reached this level of education. Educational achievement is strongly correlated to income; this rise in the American educational level, initiated by the GI Bill, has contributed directly to our improved standard of living. The GI Bill was a spectacular success, with results that far exceeded the vision and intent of its framers.

It Takes Two: Both Mechanistic And Organic

The example of the GI Bill does not suggest that the framers of the bill were misguided or wrong in what they designed or expected. Rather, their nuts-and-bolts bill was embraced on a scale that created positive consequences far beyond its original purpose. The outcome would never have been achieved from bottom-up efforts alone; the resources to create these opportunities had to be centrally gathered and directed; mechanistic forces initiated the effort. But at the receiving end, where the resources were applied, sufficient autonomy allowed the recipients to adjust to their specific situations and needs and to succeed brilliantly. With resources made available, millions of independent decisions at the organic level made the GI Bill an amazing success. This is an example of the sweet spot between mechanistic and organic forces, where these two forces reinforce each other and create results that could be described as a sum greater than its parts.

Just as a successful individual leader needs to complement the authority given to him or her (mechanistic) with his or her abilities to influence followers (organic), so should organizations constantly search for the best balance of top-down direction and bottom-up execution.

While the GI Bill is one example with favorable outcomes, not all directed programs or grassroots efforts have had such noble intentions or beneficial results. Organic habits and customs can be vicious; many exclusionary attitudes (tribalism, racism, hatred of the bourgeoisie, etc.) are often deeply embedded *within* cultures, not directed from above. Sometimes it takes a lightning bolt from higher levels to begin the change process, to erode organic attitudes in need of drastic revision. President

Harry Truman's Executive Order 9981 of 1948, which officially ended racial discrimination in the United States armed services, did not change attitudes overnight, but it did set the unmistakable tone for significant institutional revisions that gradually did change attitudes and made significant progress over the decades that followed.

Complementary, But Not Symmetric

While mechanistic and organic forces are complementary in the best conditions, they are never perfectly symmetrical. One key difference is time: mechanistic actions can be made quickly. Hence the perpetual appeal of the hero or "man on horseback" to come in, clarify things, clean up the mess, and point the way forward. In contrast, most organic actions, by their decentralized nature, require greater periods to coalesce and take effect. Discerning patterns and trends in dispersed organic actions requires both more time and more effort than in mechanistic, top-down decisions. Perhaps one of the great breakthroughs in digital information, especially "big data," will be the ability to identify trends more rapidly from dispersed actions that comprise organic forces. Perhaps this will help my stock portfolio, since the workings of the free market, such as stock exchanges, are classic examples of organic forces.

Because of the imbalance of time, with organic forces consuming more time to reveal their impact than mechanistic forces, a common cause of organizational failure is blind faith in the effectiveness of top-down decisions. A frequent example is a top-down directive that ignores the challenges of organic implementation. Admittedly, not all hierarchical decisions depend on an organic response. For example, some top-down directives require only compliance with a decision made at the top, such as raising the price of a product. Here, the organizational response relies only on information, not on actions involving judgment in execution. In our increasingly complex world, however, many directives from above will be behavior-dependent in implementation; that is, success in execution will depend on the judgment of those carrying out the directive.[10] This

---

[10] I have taken the concepts of decision-driven change and behavior-dependent change from Smith, Douglas K. *Taking Charge of Change: 10 Principles for Managing People and Performance. Reading,* MA: Addison-Wesley Pub. Co., 1996, pg. 7.

dependence occurs in all organizational and societal endeavors, whether tactical (initiating cross-selling, improving performance incrementally, improving a public service), operational (adopting new software or creating standardized electronic health records), or strategic (entering new markets, developing new products, overhauling taxation at the government level). Before undertaking any effort that requires human judgment in execution, a careful assessment of organic implementation challenges is a requirement, not an add-on or afterthought.

The old adage, "Hope is not a method," applies most profoundly to complementing a top-down directive with its organic execution. Mechanistic/organic imbalances on a grand scale have had disastrous consequences throughout our five millennia of recorded history. Perhaps the most graphic examples of this failure are in military history, for a military plan is only successful if the military unit carrying out the plan is capable of executing it. During World War I, one of the first dramatic developments was the frequent failure of the Austro-Hungarian Army to achieve success on its own. (It only achieved military success when bolstered by its German ally.) Some historians describe the architect of this disaster, Austro-Hungarian Chief of Staff Franz Conrad von Hötzendorf, as a strategic genius for his bold plans. I conclude that such judgments are just intellectual parlor games; his plans were fantasy because his army could not execute them. This disconnect caused severe losses of Austro-Hungarian soldiers fighting the Russian Army, especially talented officers, at the outset of the war—losses from which the already-stumbling Austro-Hungarian Army never recovered. That was not the work of a genius; it was gross incompetence. Poets may encourage our reach to exceed our grasp, but that is terrible advice for fighting a war.[11]

Why This Balance Matters: Cumulative Improvement Is The Lifeblood of Our Society

Conrad von Hötzendorf's failure to align his plans with the reality of his army's capabilities not only put his army "on the ropes" for the rest of the war; it also directly contributed to the demise of his country.

---

[11] Browning, Robert. "Andrea Del Sarto." Poetry Foundation. https://www.poetryfoundation.org/poems/43745/andrea-del-sarto.

The Austro-Hungarian Empire was dismantled at the end of World War I. Clearly, achieving the right balance between directed effort (top-down, mechanistic) and the level of individuals and small groups who must figure out how to get it done (organic) is essential for increasing the probabilities of success. How do we know if we are achieving this balance? What does success look like?

Certainly, sustained and measured performance is a direct indication of success. But I suggest that we look beyond even that for something deeper. The fundamental goal of our leadership efforts should go beyond accomplishing the desired goal; embedded in that success should be *cumulative improvement*, the lifeblood of our capacity to improve. When working together, we should ask ourselves, with each iteration of a task, at every level: Have we, at a minimum, made it easier to perform this task the next time? More broadly, have we learned to make our efforts more effective, more efficient, or both going forward? This advanced approach offers success at the organic level. This is not a nice-to-have; it is a must-have for continued success, as opposed to mere survival.

The constant desire to promote cumulative improvement must be ingrained in what we do because we are dependent on progress in our current age. In the West, this progress began on a sustained basis 500 years ago with the Age of Discovery and the invention of the printing press and accelerated profoundly with industrialization. The most striking proof of acceleration is the increase in the world's population from only one billion around 1800 to more than seven billion today. In the past two centuries we have spectacularly improved our material condition (especially food production and transportation); otherwise, we could never have supported such a dramatic increase in population.

But our *material* condition is much easier to improve than our *behavioral* condition, probably because we must completely change out our human talent with each generation and relearn hard lessons. Still, we have made some real progress in human behavior—our world is demonstrably less violent than in centuries past, our collective education level is higher, and we enjoy the great gift of leisure time, for example.

Nevertheless, progress in human behavior is much slower and often more unsteady than technological and material progress, and we can revert back to destructive behavior very quickly, as the bloody first half of the twentieth century so vividly showed.

In the past 200 years, people building on the accomplishments of others have advanced both our material condition (indisputably) and our behavioral condition (more haltingly, and still very fragile) through industrialization. And the most significant driver of cumulative improvement—innovation—finds its deepest roots in organic forces, not in mechanistic ones.

Our Most Organic Product: Innovation

Who began the Industrial Revolution? Probably the best answer is that it began when a number of owners of coal mines in Britain wanted to get water out of their mines because they were digging deeper to get coal to sell as fuel (the supply of wood for fuel had been depleted in England). That need, coupled with a newfangled device running on steam power that pumped water, began a long series of connections, a series of interrelated cumulative improvements, that provided new sources of energy for the first time in history.

Perhaps a more penetrating question is: Who *didn't* start the Industrial Revolution? The list is long, but most prominently it should contain the two ancient universities of England (Oxford and Cambridge) and the government of the United Kingdom. These great institutions certainly piggybacked on the Industrial Revolution as it gathered steam, but they did not direct its initiation.[12] The most significant advance in the human material condition since the advent of farming ten thousand years ago, therefore, was *not* directed from above; it evolved from below. The beginning of the Industrial Revolution was far more organic than the confusing "organic" labels on various foods in the supermarkets today.

Innovation is derived from the Latin verb *innovare*, which means to renew or change. In my use of the word innovation, I wish to imply a

---

[12] While the UK government did not direct this incredible change effort, the underlying stability of the nation and the existence of the rule of law, especially patent protection, were critical for establishing a foundation for change.

positive direction, an improvement, either by introducing something radically new (something tangible or a process) or by improving on something incrementally. The remarkable trail of innovation since the beginning of the Industrial Revolution more than 200 years ago shows one consistent theme: The process was driven by individuals and small groups acting on their own, not being directed by some grand plan. And in all cases, self-interest was never too far from the surface. The pursuit of self-interest was a huge factor in the success of the Industrial Revolution, but this self-interest was effectively channeled within the broader effects of industrialization—those larger forces that benefitted society on a large scale. To illustrate this channeling, let us examine two forces which linked self-interest to the trend of overall cumulative improvement: the first was patent law, which protected individual innovation (and reward) for a certain period (after which others could utilize innovations); the second was a gradual recognition that potential growth from innovation would produce benefits on a massive scale—for both supply and demand. A synergy between self-interest and large-scale improvement developed, rare in human history.

How does this relate to leadership? A similar mutually advantageous combination of the leader's self-interest and the benefit to the group is the ideal goal. This entire essay assumes that followers have choices. In relatively free societies, followers have discretion about how much effort they invest in any endeavor. Followers can "get by" and exert just enough effort to avoid adverse attention. Or, followers can apply themselves and give additional effort to increase the endeavor's probability of success. This *discretionary effort* is what separates mere compliance from engagement.[13] The use of force can squeeze out grudging obedience and spurts of action, but only *inspiring leadership* achieves discretionary effort. This discretionary effort (which cannot be decreed from above), when encouraged in a fertile organizational culture, is the source of cumulative improvement in that endeavor. The mark of an inspiring leader is the ability to obtain this discretionary effort from followers.

---

[13] I first learned of the concept of discretionary effort from Colonel (US Army, retired) William L. Wilson, formerly of the Department of Behavioral Science and Leadership, the United States Military Academy, in a conversation in 1996.

In my taxonomy of leadership, *inspiring leadership* is the highest level. It is rare and only occurs with a fortunate combination of leaders and situations. But we can develop leaders to reach the level of *capable leaders*, a more general level of consistency so that they can be ready to rise up to be inspiring leaders when conditions allow. Let us now explore the elements of leadership that capable leaders must possess.

CHAPTER 4

The Key Elements Of Leadership

THE PREVAILING POPULAR VIEWS: *"Leadership is about the X factor—as long as you have [fill in the blank with the latest fad], you can lead." "Management is about bean counting, but leadership is cool."*

TOUGH LOVE REALITIES: *Leadership is a complex combination of factors, both internal (the leader) and external (the context). Management and leadership are different but*  *overlapping concepts, and, in the best cases, are mutually reinforcing. One key difference: management is eminently scalable, while leadership in its purest form is, in most circumstances, not scalable.*

What are the essential elements of effective leadership? Before I attempt to address this question, I must confess how unhelpful much of the leadership literature I have read in the past fifty years has generally been. The least helpful genre is the "I've been really successful, and here is how I did it" approach. These books are usually stream-of-consciousness paeans of self-congratulation, wherein every success was self-driven; no mention of luck or probability appears in these self-marketing tools. The second unhelpful genre is the laundry list, with a mind-numbing collection of traits and abilities, often not well organized, which exceeds our mental capacity to retain.

As a contrarian, I have endeavored to focus on what makes people motivated to *follow* a leader, and still address the basic question: What should leaders *do* to be effective? If we assume that behaviors are observable actions, what are the *behaviors* of an effective leader? Since human beings are inherently complex as individuals, and even more complex in interactions with one another, can we develop a basic model to help frame fundamental principles of effective leadership behavior, despite the complexity of the subject?

A Model That's Not Perfect—But Good Enough

Distilling the essence of effective leadership into a basic model is the challenge facing anyone engaged in this complex phenomenon. Some maintain that any attempt to reduce leadership to a simplified model is a fool's errand. But my experience has been that, no matter how quixotic this effort may appear, it is always worthwhile to clarify complex subjects. At a minimum, the effort can establish a basic vocabulary to enable consistency in the discussion. More importantly, a good model can provide structure to enable the practitioner to make sense of events, to categorize behaviors rather than perceiving them as simply random occurrences. Most importantly, a model can guide leadership development, giving a framework for developing and assessing leaders, an endeavor too often left to chance in organizations today.

For the past fifty years (since entering the United States Military Academy, West Point, in 1968) I have been trying to develop a basic model of the key elements of leadership. The military culture provides an excellent laboratory for this quest: Commissioned and noncommissioned officers are given leadership responsibilities at a very early age, including leading people from a wide variety of backgrounds (an opportunity I have found not as common in many aspects of the current business world). During the twenty years I served in the US Army as an officer, including in combat, I had the privilege of leading under many different circumstances, including leading my subordinate leaders. Equally importantly, I was being led by a variety of leaders. In my business career, I continued my leadership experiences, once again by leading and being led, and also by comparing the two cultures, business and military. Throughout this combined career, I was always asking questions: what makes this person so effective or ineffective as a leader, and from these examples, what can I do to be more effective as a leader?

My Leadership Model

My hand was forced when I was tasked with the responsibility to create the leadership development program for the consulting firm where I worked in the late 1990s. In a very practical way, I now had to crystalize what leaders must do. By combing the leadership literature and comparing it to my own experiences, I went through a series of different leadership models. I took ideas from a variety of sources (cited and described in the Notes at the end of this book) and tried to create a leadership model in the "sweet spot" between complexity and simplicity; that is, basic and easy to remember, but comprehensive, able to cover most situations.

After many iterations and applications, I thought I'd nailed it. I came up with three key elements derived from the leadership behaviors that many studies say followers react to most favorably. This was my Leadership Triad. I even hedged my bets by establishing the importance of the specific organizational context of the leader and followers, to give my model a wide range of applications. Just as Athena jumped, fully grown and fully armed, from the brow of Zeus in Greek myths, my Leadership Model was ready to take on the world.

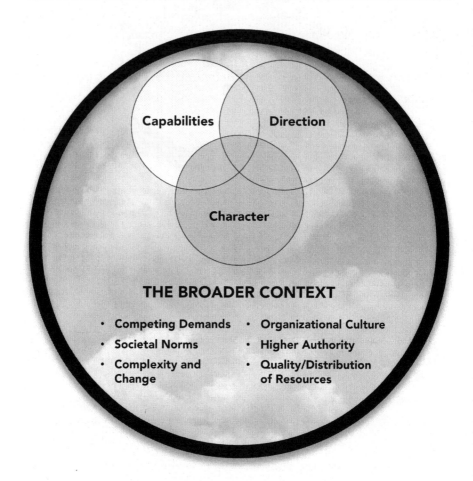

THE BROADER CONTEXT

- Competing Demands
- Societal Norms
- Complexity and Change
- Organizational Culture
- Higher Authority
- Quality/Distribution of Resources

The Context Of My Model

What I sought to develop in my model was not a formula, but a set of principles to apply across a wide range of circumstances. The model shows the triad of key leadership elements: the actions and behaviors of the leader that affect followers—*direction, capabilities,* and *character*—displayed here as overlapping circles because these elements frequently intersect. These elements are not floating abstractions, however. When the three elements of the triad are examined in detail, they always must be considered within the context of the leader's broader environment. The broader context, shown in black as a ring of iron, binds these elements. This ring represents the specific context, the unique situation, in which the leader must attempt to affect others to achieve the organizational goal, with the six bullets showing the most common "outside" factors that can influence the leader's success.

It is this inevitable variation of contexts, the complexity of the environments in which we try to lead, that render glib leadership solutions ("it's all about collaboration") unhelpful, and makes many unfiltered, self-congratulatory individual accounts ("Here's how I did it") impractical for any applications beyond the special circumstances of an author's individual experience within a specific context. As mere mortals trying to lead, we must carefully assess the context in which we lead and be constantly alert to changes in that context. In most situations, to be effective, the leader must adjust some of his or her elements to fit the context, rather than rigidly forcing a formula, a set of tools, or a specific style onto the context in the vain hope that the context will conform to the individual leader.

The Inner Context: The Larger Organization

We all operate within some larger sphere of activity. If we lead within a large organization, we will be frequently reminded of the presence of the organizational levels above us. If we operate in a small business, we are part of the larger set of similar enterprises in that industry. In a family, we have a set of experiences and stories that surround us and influence us. In short: all organizations and collections of enterprises have *cultures*.

My working definition of "culture" is *the enduring set of beliefs and assumptions within the organization that determine how things actually get done.*[14] Culture is the rock upon which most formulaic interpretations of leadership are shattered. Those enduring beliefs and assumptions are often quite different from the idealized values posted on the wall in the break room. Leaders (especially leaders new to an organization) must play anthropologist to discover the *real* values that drive actions within the organization. In some cases, the aspiring leader may conclude that the real organizational values—which create its collective culture—are simply

---

[14] For my definition of "culture" I have borrowed from Edgar H. Schein's definition in his book *Organizational Culture and Leadership*, second edition. Jossey-Bass, San Francisco: 1992. On page 12, he writes, "The culture of a group can now be defined as: A pattern of shared basic assumptions that the group learned as it solved problems of external adaptation and internal integration, that has worked well enough to be considered valid and, therefore, to be taught to new members as the correct way to perceive, think, and feel in relation to those problems."

too contrary to his or her own individual values, and he or she should then exercise the benefit of free choice and depart from the organization.

> **Culture is the rock upon which most formulaic interpretations of leadership are shattered.**

Bosses Matter: Higher Authority

One clue about organizational values comes from observations of the behavior of those in higher positions. Our natural penchant to focus on those with higher status means that the behavior of those above us can influence behavior in a cascading fashion through the organization, for good or ill. Assessing your relationship with your boss also requires dispelling a persistent myth: You don't lead your boss. Or to put it in a slightly more nuanced manner, no boss perceives him- or herself as being led by a subordinate.

Authority based on hierarchy means that bosses are not consciously looking for the people they lead to lead *them*. Within the levels of leaders in a hierarchy, the subordinate can certainly *influence* the boss, but that skill is not leadership. This suggests an answer to the age-old question (often asked by followers about their superior): "How in the world did he or she ever get there?" The answer: the skill of ingratiating yourself to your boss can be very distinct from your ability to lead your followers. This is especially true in large organizations.

The challenge to a leader in a multi-tiered hierarchy is to demonstrate the ability to lead assigned followers while also influencing the boss in a positive manner. *But the irony (and the depressing reality) is that leadership ability does not automatically transfer to effectively influencing the boss.* I have observed many instances of highly capable leaders who were not effective in influencing their own bosses, and in many cases, their success as leaders could not override this deficiency. This dilemma has played out in history several times. During the Second World War, the US Army had more than one outstanding combat division commander (a major general commanding a unit of about 15,000 soldiers) who was relieved of command, not from incompetence, but because of friction with his superior.[15]

This influence-the-boss challenge can be further complicated when a boss is envious of a subordinate's leadership ability. In our current age of anxiety about job security, survival instincts can drive superiors to fear competent subordinates who might, in some real or imagined way, overshadow the boss. We need to face the sad fact that some leaders are uncomfortable with outstanding subordinate leaders. The depressing reality is that keeping your head down, "doing a great job" as a leader, assuming that this will be rewarded, is seldom enough to achieve success within the organization. The relationship with the boss, especially the immediate boss, is crucial. Extending your influence up the organizational chain is not directly leading, per se, but it is an essential skill for survival.

The irony of leadership, especially within a large hierarchy, is that the relationship with the immediate boss is in many cases the most important relationship for individual success and promotion, *but this success is often disconnected from the ability to lead.* Leadership effectiveness is actually best revealed in the behavior of the leader's subordinates, but all too often, the higher boss is content to assess the subordinate leader based only on that leader's relationship with him or her.

Resources: Know What You've Got

Other vexing aspects of the organizational context are the quality of resources you possess (especially human resources) and competing demands for resources within the organization. Millions of people have read or seen the story related by retired US Navy Captain, L. David Marquet, describing his experience as commander of the submarine, SSN *Santa Fe*.[16] It is an inspiring story about how he was trained to command a specific type of submarine, but at the last minute was instead given command of the *Santa Fe,* a very different type of sub. He discovered that the Navy's top-down command-and-control approach did not work

---

[15] Two examples from the European Theater were the relieving of Major General Terry Allen, Commander of the 1st Infantry Division and of Major General John S. "P" Wood, Commander of the 4th Armored Division. Both were outstanding combat leaders who created friction with their superiors and were removed.

[16] Marquet, David. "How Great Leaders Serve Others." TEDxScottAFB. YouTube. June 21, 2012. Accessed February 08, 2019. https://youtu.be/DLRH5J_93LQ.

well in this new context because he was unfamiliar with the systems of the submarine. As a result, he delegated significant control and responsibilities to his subordinates; the submarine and crew performed splendidly. It is an inspiring story with elements relating to organic and mechanistic approaches, but it also emphasizes the importance of context for any leadership situation. While Captain Marquet was unfamiliar with his sub's systems, his crew was well trained. Their skill level allowed him to devolve responsibility, and Captain Marquet knew this; after all, we don't want a bunch of amateurs running nuclear-powered submarines.

Devolve Responsibility—Very Carefully

Marquet's example shows that you should assign responsibility only down to a level where it can be competently handled. Devolving responsibility never means "anything goes" or "we'll just learn from our mistakes."

On one of my first consulting assignments, I was fortunate to work with a very experienced executive in the oil industry. We were discussing the downstream aspects of the industry, specifically refining, as well as leaders at a refinery. I slipped into "consultant-ese" and uttered some cliché about giving subordinates room to make mistakes. This executive stopped me immediately. "No!" he said. "In this business, I want him to do *exactly* what he is supposed to do. Otherwise, things can blow up."

I have always been grateful for that response. There are a number of time-tested processes and procedures to reduce risk, and these are not arenas for the exercise of creativity.

More fundamentally, subordinates must possess and demonstrate basic skills before the leader encourages wider ranges of independent judgment. Leaders must quickly assess the levels of skill within their group, for those skill levels determine the overall capability of the group and the degree of oversight required. The leader must make this assessment quickly by observing performance, not taking their self-assessments at face value. We humans are notoriously bad at assessing our own skills; we tend to grossly overrate ourselves.[17] Therefore, a gimlet eye is an essential

---

[17] DeAngelis, Tori. "Why We Overestimate Our Competence." American Psychological Association. *Monitor on Psychology*, February 2003, Vol. 34, no. 2. https://www.apa.org/monitor/feb03/overestimate. Perhaps our tendency to overrate our own abilities is best expressed by Garrison Keillor in his description of Lake Wobegon, where "all the children are above average."

tool for the leader to gauge subordinates' skill levels. And we cannot let our current culture's celebration of creativity blind us. Yes, we love to see individual creativity in our entertainment, but every time we fly on an aircraft, we want the maintenance crew to have done *exactly* what they were supposed to do.

Competing Demands

The final vexing aspect of the organizational context is where the leader's activity rates within the priorities of the larger organization. It's great to be at the heart of the endeavor, where the "real work" gets done, but we're not always so lucky; we may be the stagehands instead of the lead actors. A supporting role often draws less attention, praise, and resources, which can create greater challenges for those who lead such groups. Secondary roles, responsible for activities that fit lower in the pecking order, are usually understood by all involved, even if they are not explicitly expressed. To keep a group engaged in a supporting role motivated, the leader must ensure that they comprehend their role in the bigger picture and how they will contribute to ultimate success.

The interlocking importance of different roles within a larger effort was conveyed to me in a conversation with Sir Edgar Williams, CB, CBE, DSO, who, as a Brigadier in the British Army, was Field Marshal Montgomery's intelligence officer during World War II. While visiting Sir Edgar in the early 1980s, I asked him what had been the decisive factor in their victory over Erwin Rommel, the German general also known as "Desert Fox," in North Africa. I expected an answer describing some tactical advantage in equipment or training, or a brilliant strategic insight. "Fruit," he replied with a smile; he knew the answer would catch me off guard. Confused, I asked him to explain. He proceeded to tell me the superiority of their supply system gave the British a much better diet than the Germans. He said disease was terrible in North Africa, but the British suffered less than the Germans because they had a better diet. Sir Edgar's insights reminded me that in all the moving parts of a huge effort, you'd best have effective leaders in *all* roles, even the roles that gain less attention.

I doubt if there was ever a war movie made in which the lead was a supply officer, but I am eternally grateful that the Allies had such well-placed talent in World War II.

The Bigger Picture: Societal Norms

Beyond the realm of the larger organization itself, a bigger set of cultural artifacts exists—the norms, or standards of behavior, of the society at large. While anthropologists tell us that many characteristics are common to all cultures, our experiences working with people in global organizations often accentuate the differences. Especially when working in a culture different from your own, the leader must understand this context and how it will affect his or her ability to lead.

Differences can be truly global, from truck drivers in the Middle East turning a three-lane highway into a five-lane highway, to clients in East Asia valuing *more* gray hair while Westerners try everything to hide it. Cultural differences can also be found within regions—for example, differences in punctuality standards among Germans, English, and Spanish. They can even be local—don't wear a Yankees baseball cap in Boston.

These pervasive norms will influence the impact of the leader's values on the group. As I will discuss shortly, *character* (one of the three key elements of leadership) is the set of values that each of us carries that determines our behavior. When the collective set of values in the larger context (group or society norms) differs from the leader's own set of values, either some sort of accommodation is required, or the relationship will not hold. It is difficult to alter the values of the larger society or group, so the burden of making adjustments often rests with the leader. Therefore, the leader's initial assessment of the group's values is crucial to determine areas of potential friction.

The Biggest Context: Change And Complexity

But wait!

If we live in such an age of change and I am saying that societies don't change their values easily, how can that be? The answer is that our current age of change is actually overrated. I believe we vastly exaggerate change in our current era. Conduct this exercise: Trace your family tree, if you can, and go back four or five generations (depending on your current age). Go back to an ancestor born around 1860. Compare the changes that that person experienced during his or her lifetime compared to you. I have done this exercise with myself and others, and the overwhelming conclusion was, our ancestors who lived through the first period of industrialization (in the United States, roughly from 1860 to 1920) not only endured profound technological change, but significant *behavioral* change as well. Moving from agrarian work to industrial work changed the sense of time from seasonal progression to the daily clock. Agrarian work was decentralized, the opposite of centralized industrial work. Today we have but the faintest sense of how profound these changes were. I was born in 1950, and in my lifetime, I have experienced nothing like the changes experienced by my great-grandfather, Arthur Lupfer (1857–1957), which I will discuss in detail in Chapter 11.

I am not suggesting that we are not undergoing important changes today, especially in technology. But the most profound technological change in my lifetime, digitization, has not yet run its course, and its impact will increase well beyond my lifetime. I have not yet seen the same degree of change in *behavior* today that industrialization brought two or three generations before mine. We must remember that, since the Industrial Revolution, technological change is cumulative, with changes that build on previous changes, moving at an accelerated pace. Changes in human *behavior* have not progressed in such a neat, upward path. Therefore, I recommend that we not treat change as the media currently treat unusual weather events—portents of the end of days. To understand the larger context with regard to change, I encourage leaders to assess the impact of changing technology (especially digitization), but also to recall that human nature has remained more consistent and predictable.

As a consequence, rapid technological change often runs up against the glacier-like movements of human nature. With digitization, we enjoy access to significantly greater amounts of information than we ever imagined in the past. Unfortunately, we still have the same human brain, which dislikes complexity and wants simplicity. Ironically, in the midst of an explosion of information, a leader's ability to simplify with reasonable (not perfect) accuracy is becoming even more essential now than in the past. As our environments and challenges have become more complex, the need for a fundamental, practical model for what leaders should do becomes more pressing. My set of three key elements for effective leadership form the core of such a leadership model.

The First Element: Direction

To address the first of the three elements in my model, the element of *direction* means, first, that the leader must articulate the organization's and specific group's goals clearly and then determine if they are understood and adopted by the members of the group. To apply this approach to a specific situation, in the current American business environment, we see weak individual loyalty to institutions due to, among other factors, weak loyalty of institutional leadership to their employees, resulting in much greater individual movement across different organizations. As a result, leaders must recognize that an individual follower's goals may have a shorter time horizon than the broader organizational goals. By understanding that specific context, the leader can determine the mix of self-interest and aspiration that he or she must use to effectively frame organizational goals for the members of the group to gain their commitment. For example, a member of the group may not intend to stick around to see the results of a five-year expansion, but he or she will probably respond to more short-term benefits, such as gaining personal experience and development during the initial phase.

Large organizations often enjoy consistent, predictable goals, but newer, smaller organizations face a greater challenge in defining direction. The leader of a start-up must devote a significant effort to defining and refining the purpose and direction of the endeavor. One of the recurring mistakes in the early stages of any enterprise is to try to be all things to all potential customers. The leader's clarity about what the enterprise is (and, equally importantly, what it is *not*) often determines the difference between success and failure for new endeavors. False starts, distractions, novelties, and fads occur much more frequently than The Next Big Thing, and the effective leader must communicate to followers what must be done to stay on point.

Building The Cathedral

Besides using the authority of position to define the direction and set priorities for group efforts, the effective leader should link followers' efforts to the greater purpose. Motivation is a complex and often mysterious aspect of human behavior, but evidence indicates that, while material rewards are effective in the short run, they tend to be short-lived.[18] The most enduring motivators tend to be more emotional than tangible. A very powerful example of an enduring motivator is to be engaged in meaningful work, work that serves a clear purpose. Effective leaders put work in context for followers to show where and how their efforts contribute to the larger purpose. This is particularly important for efforts in perceived secondary roles. Leaders skilled in the key element, *direction*, can reveal how even the most mundane effort serves the larger purpose, which generates stronger engagement in their followers.

A story (probably apocryphal) tells of Sir Christopher Wren visiting the work site of his great masterpiece, St. Paul's Cathedral in London, in the seventeenth century. The workmen with whom he spoke did not recognize him, so they honestly answered his question, "What are you doing?" The first said he was cutting a stone; the second said he was earning his pay; the third said he was helping Sir Christopher Wren build a great cathedral. To look at this engaging story through a realistic lens, we must acknowledge that the three motivations—performing a task, earning a wage, and working toward a larger purpose—are not mutually exclusive. We probably all shuttle between them in any work we do. But the leader who can employ *direction* to remind followers periodically of how their efforts fit into the larger picture can strike an important emotional chord.

---

[18] Piekema, Carinne. "Does Money Really Motivate People?" *BBC Future*. BBC, November 18, 2014. Accessed May 29, 2019. http://www.bbc.com/future/story/20120509-is-it-all-about-the-money.
See also Riggio, Ronald F. "5 Reasons Why Money Is a Poor Work Motivator." *Psychology Today*. Sussex Publishers, May 3, 2018. https://www.psychologytoday.com/us/blog/cutting-edge-leadership/201805/5-reasons-why-money-is-poor-work-motivator.

"Every calling is great when greatly pursued."
—OLIVER WENDELL HOLMES JR.

Regrettably, the term "engagement" is sadly overworked in today's discussions of the workplace, but if we can overcome its cliché status, we can see that the skillful employment of direction, providing context to give greater meaning to work, can foster engagement and commitment, from which can come the greatest gift from followers: their discretionary effort. Achieving this elevates *capable* leadership to *inspiring* leadership.

The Second Element: Capabilities

Turning to the next element of the leadership model triad, *capabilities* means the skills and knowledge *appropriate for the leader's position in the organization* which the leader employs to achieve the organizational goals, or, quite simply, managerial ability.

Much ink has been spilled parsing differences between *management* and *leadership*. One of my contrarian views is that these concepts are not diametrically opposed; rather, whereas they may differ significantly in the sense of scale, they should be mutually reinforcing concepts for individual and organizational success.

Here is my working definition of management:

Management is the employment of all resources to achieve the organizational goals.

The key difference between management and leadership is that management involves *all* resources at one's disposal. A working list of the basic resources that must be managed is:

- Time
- Tangibles (materials, equipment, facilities)
- Processes
- Financial resources
- Relationships (often with people you are *not* leading, such as a boss, customers, regulators, etc.)

- Information (including data and communications)
- People

Management is a broad concept, covering all resources that can be "handled"—the Latin root word for "hand" is "man" or "manu," the basis for our word "manage." Leadership is much narrower. The only resource one directly leads is people. Management has an impact on a leader's success because proficient management is a major part of the leader's capability to operate at the assigned level.

Management also differs from leadership because management is about *scale*: the higher the decision-making role, the greater the resources to manage, and the broader the impact. We need the top managers to be the best managers at the highest levels. *Leadership, by contrast, is limited in scale.* Under most conditions, a leader can only touch so many people emotionally, regardless of position in the hierarchy. This may sound completely insane: Your top leader may not be your *best* leader. Consider the example of leadership in war: The most challenging leadership roles are

> **Management is the employment of all resources to achieve the organizational goals.**

those where people face the existential threat of dying. This is the realm of sergeants, lieutenants, and captains. Generals should not be facing these threats in most situations; they are in their positions to manage the *resources* necessary to achieve victory, to lead (in the pure leadership sense) their *immediate* subordinates, and to provide a solid example for the members of the larger organization. Management operates at scale, and the managerial talent should match the scale—the higher one goes, the more capable he or she must be. Leadership, as opposed to management, is more dispersed and *personal*—you need capable leaders at all levels, and you should strive to have inspiring leaders, but the person at the top does *not* have to be the ultimate über-leader.

Management ability is important in all positions, including the specialist, because resources are employed in any activity we undertake.

This is why the specialist can be crucial for organizational success without assuming the role of a leader (other than exercising indirect leadership through reputation). But for the smaller group of leaders within the organization, those people whose role establishes a direct relationship between leader and followers, leadership and management are always intertwined, and under the best conditions, are mutually reinforcing. The capability to employ resources effectively (management) is critical for a leader's success. No one wants to follow a failure or an incompetent. When leading that crucial resource—humans—management and leadership abilities overlap, for the leader *manages* people through processes and *leads* people by direct interaction.

Management and Leadership Reinforce Each Other: An Example

Say you are running a twenty-four-hour-a-day operation, such as a department of a hospital, and Thanksgiving is coming up. You have already established (and are managing) a process to select those who will work on Thanksgiving. By *managing* people as a key resource through this process, you have identified the "lucky" few who will work on Thanksgiving. But the week before Thanksgiving, you meet with the people tapped to work on Thanksgiving (which they've known for several weeks since you have managed the process very well) to tell them that the hospital is counting on them working the holiday, and you ask them if they have any questions or concerns.

Now you are interacting with them directly, and you are *leading* them. You are not merely asking these questions to be nice and pleasant. You've been around the block enough times to know that the last thing you want on the Wednesday evening before Thanksgiving is a call from one of them as they talk through a faked cough, telling you that they are sick and can't come in on Thanksgiving. In a very positive way, you're now reminding them of their commitment and how important it is. When you stop by the hospital yourself on Thanksgiving and seek each one out to check on them and thank them for their work, you are demonstrating *inspiring leadership*.

For those being led, the overlap between management and leadership is that followers expect their leader to be a capable manager in the position in which he or she is serving. I have observed that the importance of *capabilities*, or managerial ability, as a key element in leadership has been frequently diluted in recent years in many organizations by an overemphasis on emotional connections alone (I will discuss this phenomenon under *character*). In fact, I will go further: I believe that demonstrating *capabilities* is the prerequisite that then enables the third element, *character*, to have an effect on followers.

Reality alert: *Emotions alone will never carry the day*—the emotional connection between the leader and followers must be built on a foundation of direction and capabilities.

We learn this relationship the hard way when we are in a job where we are "in over our heads." Despite good intentions, if we do not possess the abilities required for the job, we will fail or earn a reputation for being ineffective. Few people, especially in today's anxious work environment, want to admit that they lack necessary skills and knowledge for an assigned role, and many will undertake contortions worthy of a Soviet gymnast to hide the deficiency. But a leader's lack of capability is difficult to hide from his or her core followers. Followers don't expect their leader to know every detail or have every skill required to do all the subordinates' jobs, but they do expect their leader to have the knowledge and skills required to do the *leader's* job, and they are quick to catch on when that capability is lacking.

> **Reality Alert:** *Emotions alone will never carry the day*—the emotional connection between the leader and followers must be built on a foundation of direction and capabilities.

The link between *direction* and *capabilities* is the vital path from intent to results. One dangerous way to erode the importance of capabilities as a key element in leader effectiveness is to weaken that link.

Many potential detours on that path can weaken a leader's effectiveness. A leader can become fixated on intermediate activities, engaging in a short-term activity as an end in itself, not focusing on longer-term results. In a similar vein, leaders can become enamored with process, believing that simply following a set of actions, doing *something*, shows real accomplishment irrespective of results. Organizations can err as well, communicating that leadership roles are easy; it's just "plug and lead." Downplaying the importance of a leader's raw abilities can likewise weaken the organization's obligation to identify the skills and knowledge that matter for leadership roles—an increasingly challenging task, since globalization and technology often require both broader and deeper skills and knowledge. For that reason, organizations need to devote more effort to identify the skills and knowledge that really count in critical leadership jobs—the capabilities that get results.

The Raw Desire To Succeed Is Never Enough: Capabilities Matter

As a key leadership element, *capabilities* are quite vulnerable to sudden change in context, as I once learned in retailing. In a store chain in which I worked, one of the best store managers was promoted to regional director. One of the old retailing veterans predicted that this manager would fail, and I didn't want to believe his prediction. But he was correct; this manager was outstanding running a specialty store but was lost in the new role as a director over several stores. Most organizations use the familiar heuristic that a person performing well in a subordinate position can assume the next-higher position. That is a great example of an approach that is "good enough" in many cases, but this approach has also given us Parkinson's Law and the Peter Principle.[19] To develop our leaders more effectively, we must address the unsettling risk that a promotion can place a person in a new context that demands significantly different capabilities which the newly promoted person may or may not possess.

---

[19] Parkinson's Law, where work expands so as to fill the time available for its completion, was coined by C. Northcote Parkinson in the 1950s, based on his experience in the British Civil Service. He also coined the term "injelitance" to describe people being promoted who were both incompetent and jealous. The Peter Principle is the observation that people in hierarchies will rise to their level of incompetence, expressed in the book, *The Peter Principle* by Lawrence J. Peter and Raymond Hull, William Morrow & Co: 1969.

For this reason, general laundry lists of competencies, separate from any specific organizational context, are of little use. What matters is the skills and knowledge necessary to achieve results in the specific role, and whether the newly appointed occupant possesses them; if not, how quickly he or she can acquire them; and, finally, as a last resort, who else may have those skills and knowledge for that job. Leadership is an intricate mix of the three elements: *direction* and *capabilities* must be present in the leader for the third, most important, and most elusive element, *character*, to have its impact on followers.

The Third Element: Character

In my leadership model, *character* means the set of acquired individual values that consistently influence the leader's behavior. Of the three leadership elements, character is the most closely linked to the emotions of the followers. Followers will always be touched emotionally in some manner by their leaders and vice versa. We are learning through neuroscience (especially through functional MRIs) that emotions are intertwined in our brains with our cognitive functions; therefore, the purely "rational person" is a simplification that borders on myth.[20] In other words, the ability to cleanly separate our reason from our emotions does not appear to exist, so we should work from the assumption that emotions will always play a role in behavior, for better and for worse.

Character is fully formed in each of us as we reach adulthood. The root word for "character" comes from the Greek expression "to engrave," so there is a sense of permanence regarding this leadership element; as we become adults, we carry a set of fairly permanent values that will guide our behavior. Also referring to the ancients, the importance of character in leadership in this model is a direct descendant of the classical emphasis on virtue, which celebrated habits and practices that led to the *right behavior*.

Borrowing from Jonathan Haidt's writings on moral foundations, I have taken his six foundations and distilled them into six basic values for the leader:[21]

---

[20] Damasio, Antonio. *Descartes' Error: Emotion, Reason and the Human Brain*. New York: Avon Books, 1994.

[21] Haidt, Jonathan. *The Righteous Mind: Why Good People Are Divided by Politics and Religion*. London: Pantheon, 2012.

- Fairness
- Lack of malice
- Loyalty to the group and its mission
- Deference to authority and standards (meaning that the leader acknowledges authority beyond his or her own)
- Aspiration to be unsullied (meaning a constant effort to be "clean" or "pure" in behavior)
- Encouragement of autonomy

Much more research is needed in determining the basic values that are generally shared among most people, but I propose this list as a starting point for conversations about character.

The element of character is the most potentially challenging in terms of "fit" within the organization, of adjusting to context. If the practiced values of the organization (organizational culture) and the values of the leader (character) do not reasonably match, the long-term prognosis is not good, for neither is easy to change. Examining the concept of organizational culture in finer detail, the leader's values must also resonate reasonably well with his or her followers; when values diverge, the leader is faced with a challenging task.

A Difficult Challenge: Changing The Group's Values

When a leader is charged with dramatically improving the standards and performance of a group, this frequently requires changing the values of the group, one of the most difficult leadership challenges. In this situation, the leader will almost certainly not be popular with the group. Especially in today's environment of individual sensitivity, few people like to be told they are not performing well or that their attitudes are not conducive to the group's success. If the leader's bosses have not anticipated pushback from followers and do not give the leader their full support, the needle of the group dynamics can move very quickly from manageable tension to dysfunctional obstruction.

A close friend accepted a new job with a company in which he was given the mission to move the group to a higher standard as quickly as possible. The followers consisted of highly educated specialists who were extremely reluctant to change. My friend's bosses had not anticipated the inevitable tension; the bosses ultimately gave in to the griping specialists and fired my friend. In doing so, they committed two grave errors: they deprived their company of the talent and character of my friend, and they left the organizational challenge unresolved and made necessary change more difficult. Even in the best of circumstances, having the full support of higher management, the leader with the mission of raising standards or changing behavior will face considerable challenges from the impacted followers.

Trust Is The Glue

One key emotional aspect of character, more nuanced than the false hope of getting along with everyone, should be top-of-mind for the leader as he or she assesses challenges: trust, the most important by-product of all three key elements (direction, capabilities, and especially character) working in concert. Trust is the mutual reinforcement of the three key elements among leader and followers: all participants in the endeavor have general agreement about direction, respect each other's capabilities, and share common values.

Numerous studies indicate that trust is probably the most important attitude to foster in followers for a leader's long-term success. The leader's organizational status will generate some initial trust among the followers through their basic acceptance of positional authority, but this capital can be built upon or squandered quickly through subsequent leader behavior.

Examining how trust can be built up or diluted is an example of how to use this leadership model as a diagnostic tool. For example, a survey of subordinates that asks what leader behaviors either foster or erode trust can yield valuable insights for leaders at all levels. When I employed a form of this model in a consulting firm's design of new manager training, I conducted interviews and surveys with potential *followers* of new managers. The most consistent feedback: When a new manager took all the credit for the team's work, trust in that new manager dropped precipitously. These findings were practical insights for new managers in their leadership training and gave them real examples of effective and ineffective leadership behavior *before* they assumed the role. Long-term trust between a group and its leader is the most important goal, and this trust is solidified when the leader's behavior unifies all three leadership elements, reinforcing each other: a clear purpose provided through *direction*, demonstrated *capabilities*, and, most importantly, the values displayed through the leader's *character*.

My Model In Crisis

Years later, having refined my three-element model, I tested it with colleagues and through presentations with different groups. I was getting excellent feedback until I made a presentation with a very experienced group. They challenged me: If character is so important for successful leadership, why do we have so many examples of poor leaders, even (or especially) those in high positions? One person offered a specific example of a well-known executive who was notorious for being a "bad guy" to work for, and yet people still lined up to work for him. The group agreed that I had created a great working model for ideal leaders, but it fell short when exposed to reality. They were right in presenting these challenges, and I was crushed.

I tried to summon my inner Bolshevik, to bend reality to fit my model, but that didn't work. Then I began to realize that maybe we look for our best leaders in the wrong places. Perhaps a high position does not always correlate with leadership ability—a truly contrarian thought. I had to explore why bad leadership not only exists, but often prospers.

CHAPTER 5

Where Did I Go Wrong?

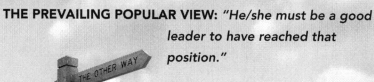

THE PREVAILING POPULAR VIEW: *"He/she must be a good leader to have reached that position."*

TOUGH LOVE REALITY: *Not necessarily. Unfortunately, effective leadership may not even be a criterion for reaching a high position in some organizations.*

The Dilemma

Here was the challenge: My model showed what leaders *should* be—people in positions of authority who give *direction* so that the group's combined efforts can achieve shared goals, who possess *capabilities* to perform effectively in their role, and, most importantly, whose *character* reveals the values that inspire followers and build trust. But (and it was a big *but*) how do I explain the many, many examples of leaders in high places who are notoriously poor leaders?

As I was licking my wounds, I realized that I should have anticipated this challenge, because I had experienced this phenomenon in both my military and business careers. How could I have forgotten my own experience as a speechwriter for a very high-ranking general? This general had a public persona as a thoughtful, careful leader, not prone to excitement or overreaction. But within his inner circle, he behaved quite differently. He was extremely temperamental and unpredictable. He would turn viciously on his subordinates for no apparent reason, and he seemed to enjoy making other human beings miserable. His only way of motivating was by inducing fear. Only one or two people had served him consistently through the years, and while most of their skills seemed to be average at best, they excelled at demonstrating a slavish devotion to the general. The rest of the staff was hired help that turned over every couple of years, and we frequently endured the full blast of a nasty temper, which could erupt at any time.

This general has since passed away, yet people who worked for him still shudder when they recall him today. But there is another important aspect to this story: This general was extremely successful in accomplishing his mission. He achieved his goals in an extremely important and sensitive position. The dilemma is that, while he achieved success at one level, he left a trail of broken bodies along the path—unnecessarily, in my view. This wasn't the proverbial "tough but fair" commander; he was malicious and arbitrary with his subordinates, and almost no one who worked for him would later imitate his approach to leading other human beings. Could he have succeeded as well in his position without such bad leadership toward his immediate staff? I answer with not only an unequivocal *yes*, but also maintain that he could have accomplished more, especially by providing an example for others to follow long after he was gone.

From this experience, and from similar examples I have observed (and occasionally endured) in business, I asked myself, how can these people ascend so high in an organization? How can someone whose leadership is so uninspiring rise so high?

I had come up with three possible reasons, and I should have kept these in mind as I was developing my model. Here are my three possible reasons, going in order from least depressing to most depressing.

Reason One: Happy Circumstances

The late comedian George Carlin had a great insight into our imperfect human judgment. In his "Idiot and Maniac" routine, he described how, when we are driving, we call anyone going slower than we are an idiot, and anyone speeding past us a maniac.[22] As this comedy routine points out, our judgments are based on our own position relative to others. Similarly, we attribute our success to our own efforts, and we tend to find external causes for our failures. How many books on personal success state, "Well, I was just lucky"? Not many. Yet, external, seemingly random events can have significant impact on personal success or failure, and on promotion within a large organization.

External events can propel someone into a position of authority where his or her talent flourishes. The turmoil of the French Revolution enabled a twenty-six-year-old Napoleon to command a field army, and in this instance, the cliché "The rest is history" is profoundly appropriate. Ulysses S. Grant would have been an obscure footnote in history without his rise during the Civil War. There is nothing insidious about whims of circumstance affecting success. The examples of Napoleon and Grant show that capable people can excel under lucky circumstances—but we must also remember that mediocre performers also get lucky breaks.

For every Napoleon or Grant, there are probably thousands who have landed by chance in a position that exceeded their abilities. While we must recognize the impact of random events, we should also note that, for long-term development and assessment of leaders, we should capture a span of experience that goes beyond one event, because one event alone may not reveal the full abilities of the leader. The old English saying is revealing: "Beware of heroes; the more you come to know them, the less you will think of them."

Reason Two: Diluted Hereditary Succession

For millennia, we humans have exercised a great labor-saving approach to identifying leaders: hereditary succession. This approach created significant advantages over the alternative—a bloody, violent struggle for power.

Hereditary succession provided leadership continuity and reduced strife, offered a career development path for the lucky child, and was a fairly

---

22 Carlin, George. "George Carlin—Idiot and Maniac." YouTube, June 21, 2012. Accessed February 1, 2019. https://youtube.com/watch?v=XWPCE2tTLZQ.

simple and straightforward process. There were, of course, complications now and then. In the Ottoman Empire, the existence of several wives of the sultan resulted in numerous potential successors when the reigning sultan died. For centuries, this problem was addressed by the the most ruthless (and fast-acting) son having his rivals—his half-brothers—strangled. In other situations (think of Shakespeare's history plays, such as *Richard II*), an ambitious relative would replace an incompetent ruler by invoking some ingenious hereditary connection to the throne to justify a swift and permanent removal of the current occupant.

During the past two centuries, we have moved away from hereditary succession toward a more meritorious process for selecting leaders—or have we? In the United States, many of our elections of presidents, governors, and senators clearly reflect hereditary selection, evident through numbers of elected officials with a family connection to others in elected higher office that greatly exceed random occurrence. Name recognition through heredity will continue to affect our choices, and this tendency will persist because this method of choosing is an easy, simple selection process—one of the most enduring of our "lazy defaults."

This tendency to defer to status (such as prestigious family ties) leads to the second, more depressing reason why someone may occupy a leadership position without having first demonstrated good leadership qualities: the chosen leader has name recognition that is unrelated to leadership ability. I call this general tendency *diluted hereditary succession*. For example, we are inclined in our assessments to mirror previous pronouncements that have already been made about those we now assess. If someone arrives in our organization with a reputation as the Golden Boy or Golden Gal, we will most likely accept that assessment, at least initially. Reputation or status *does* affect judgment. A similar path to immediate status is to have attended a prestigious and/or rigorous institution or training regimen. This is especially helpful for promotion if a network of powerful alumni already exists in the organization. Regrettably, such connections are never perfect predictors of performance, and no institution—religious, military, academic, or business—can guarantee the character of all its alumni. While this institutional approach to selection may make sense for a first cut based upon sheer efficiency, such distinctions should never be the overriding criteria for final selection for a leader. Yet this tendency persists.

Perhaps the most egregious example of labels and reputation clouding judgment is the case of the Cambridge Five, the graduates from Cambridge University who infiltrated various British government institutions and passed on top secret information to the Soviet Union for decades, from the 1930s to the 1960s. Their incredible luck in avoiding detection, despite numerous Soviet defectors potentially fingering them and a wealth of other evidence pointing to their betrayal of their country, was undoubtedly aided by a reluctance of their superiors and peers to accept that these "gentlemen" could be spies. One of the Cambridge Five, Kim Philby, even enjoyed the distinction of being an Officer of the Order of the British Empire and later receiving the Order of Lenin (after he defected to Moscow, many steps ahead of British intelligence). I have often wondered if he ever placed both certificates together above his mantle in Moscow in his declining years, for those two honors, side by side, were symbols of a culture that could not escape the false allure of class identity. We all have biases in our judgments, and we need constant and conscious effort to overcome them.

Reason Three: The Most Depressing Reason

In Ascending The Ladder, Leadership Doesn't Matter

But the depression induced by lucky events or overreliance on connections as possible reasons for poor leadership pales in comparison to the Prozac-demanding anxiety created by the third reason: that leadership ability is simply not a valued trait in the rise to higher levels of authority within many organizations.

My three-element model represents leadership in its fullest form, where interactions within a relatively small group (*the size of Dunbar's Number or less*) would fully reveal the leader's strengths and weaknesses— they have no place to hide their failings in any of the three elements from their followers, especially failings in character. This fundamental grouping with real relationships, like a small town where everyone knows your name, is where the purest form of leadership exists, where all three elements are clearly revealed. But that may not be the case the higher one ascends.

How can this be? Aren't people at the top of the organization supposed to be great leaders? The answer is that very often, they are *not* great leaders, *and they often don't have to be,* either to get there or to stay there. In a large organization with an extensive hierarchy, *capable leadership will only be a key criterion for advancement when it is directly and deliberately assessed.* And very often, capable leadership is *assumed* when a leader in a high position possesses good standing in other measures. Yet those measures may not be solid indicators of effective leadership.

Managing The Boss: Critical To Success, But Not Leadership

The most prominent of these potentially false measures is *managing the boss.* We all want to feel good about ourselves, and the trappings of power do not diminish that basic need, which makes an extreme form of managing the boss, flattery, very potent. Any subordinate who boosts his or her boss's ego is going to be looked upon positively. Making the boss feel good about him- or herself is not *always* an advanced form of sycophancy; all leaders should work to get along with their bosses, but both sides must grasp that this ability is not leadership.

If we are serving in the role of the higher boss, we must resist the pull of flattery as we assess the leadership of our subordinates, and that requires significant awareness and self-control. Since hierarchies, by their nature, are structures, people will learn how to advance by orienting upward. British Prime Minister Benjamin Disraeli advised, "Everyone likes flattery; and when you come to Royalty, you should lay it on with a trowel." Today, many people have done Disraeli one better and employ a front-end loader.

To reiterate, these tendencies, both to orient upward and to enjoy flattery from below, are natural inclinations in all of us. But we can't let that cloud our judgment. I have heard the advice, "Kiss up and kick down," too many times to dismiss it as mere joking. For far too many people, it works as a way to get ahead.

Leadership Greatness Doesn't Always Reside At The Top

We cannot allow our natural fixation on status to distort our understanding of leadership. The occupation of a high position in the hierarchy does not guarantee a capable leader. Ideally, capable leaders should permeate the organization at every level, especially at levels where the core effort is performed. Leaders at higher levels should certainly demonstrate capable leadership, but their most important duty is not to dominate as some form of alpha-dog super-leader, where all leadership wisdom originates from the top (a recurrent myth), but to develop a culture that fosters capable leadership in every leadership role, at all levels.

Success Hides Many Sins

The most depressing variant of the third reason for bad leadership at the top (when leadership doesn't matter) drips with irony—*organizational success can hide bad leadership*. The old saying from retailing about success, above, summarizes the reasons why bad leaders can prosper in high places. Spectacular success can occur for many reasons and leadership may not be a direct cause in all cases. Especially when the organizational scale gets well above Dunbar's Number, leaders at the top, *if they are perceived as successful*, can be neither inspiring nor capable. They can revert to a lesser level, Leadership Lite: the subject of the next chapter.

CHAPTER 6

Leadership Lite

THE PREVAILING POPULAR VIEW: *"This organization is performing splendidly. The leadership must be outstanding."*

TOUGH LOVE REALITY: *Organizations can perform very well with bad leadership, at least in the short run.*

Success Has Many Fathers: Failure Is An Orphan

What can the examples of Harvey Weinstein (the recently disgraced movie mogul) and the many occupants of the office of Grand Vizier of the Ottoman Empire reveal about why we suffer from, and yet tolerate, Leadership Lite?

Leadership Lite prospers when spectacular success is achieved but is aided and abetted by subordinates who are willing to endure great abuse, so long as they can be close to power. This diluted form of leadership can exist at any level, but is particularly pernicious in large organizations, where top leaders who practice Leadership Lite can use distance from the larger mass of followers to cultivate a favorable public image, while abusing their immediate subordinates, knowing that these subordinates are as consumed by ambition and power as they are, on the condition that success is achieved (or proclaimed). Success is the most effective cloak for character flaws.

The Strange Duality Of Leadership In Large Organizations

When the scale of leadership exceeds Dunbar's Number in large organizations, a duality emerges. First, the top leader affects the larger number of followers only in a broad sense, through reputation and image. This is driven primarily through the leadership elements of *direction* and *capabilities*, which directly drive the total effort. The large base of followers knows who the leader is, but they really don't *know* the leader, warts and all. The leader's true character is remote and unknowable to distant followers, separated from the top leader by layers of authority, physical distance, and the sheer number of followers, which renders close relationships impossible.

But the leader also has a smaller cadre of immediate subordinates and staff, and this is the second part of the scope of the Leadership Lite in the large hierarchy. This smaller circle represents the *fundamental* followers of a top leader—direct relationships that reveal, in addition to direction and capabilities, the true nature of the leader's character. This smaller circle is where the leader in a high organizational position actually exercises pure leadership, leadership with all three elements in play, rather than on a grand scale with large numbers of followers, where images can be conjured.

Success on a grand scale casts an aura of mastery upon the leader at the top. Sometimes this is appropriate, as when the leader, through his or her direction and capabilities, contributes directly to success, as the example of Napoleon demonstrates. He assumed command of a field army of Revolutionary France in 1796 at the young age of twenty-six and promptly led it to astonishing victories, and the young Napoleon was an inspiring leader. On other occasions, however, the leader at the top may simply be at the right place at the right time, when things go well. In medieval Europe, if the harvests were bountiful, the king enjoyed the perception of success. The reverse was also true—agricultural conditions were bad in France just before the Revolutions of 1789 and 1848. If some feel that, in our modern age, we have outgrown this error in weak cause-and-effect reasoning, think again—every United States President claims credit for favorable economic indicators, even though the causal factors for that economic success may be unrelated to the administration in power at that moment.

The large-scale success of the organization, therefore, will burnish the reputation of the current leader to create a brilliant shine, but such success is not irrefutable proof of outstanding leadership at the top. So, let's go to the movies.

Thank You, Thank You, Harvey Weinstein!

When I give presentations on business ethics, I use a training aid that provides rich examples every day—a daily newspaper. Armed with my copy of *The Wall Street Journal* from any given date, I can always identify at least one example of an ethical issue in business in any day's news. But at the time of this writing, a mother lode of poor leadership, abetted by power, has emerged that simply cannot be ignored: Harvey Weinstein. Perhaps the interest in this epic story of toleration of horrible leadership will have abated by the time of publication of my book, but I hope not, because the example of Harvey Weinstein is the essence of exceptional success masking hideous leadership.

Talk about success in a very tough industry—the movies that Harvey Weinstein produced have garnered eighty-one Academy Awards. He has been a forceful presence in the American movie industry for four decades. In reviewing the flood of stories that have emerged since the first allegations of his sexual misconduct and harassment emerged in October 2017, I have distilled two main points:

- Landing a role in a Harvey Weinstein movie was a big break for an aspiring star, especially for a woman. Due to the aggressive marketing of his films during award season, a star in his movies had a good chance of receiving an Oscar nomination.[23]

- Harvey Weinstein expected sexual favors in return.

---

[23] Harvey Weinstein was a master of promoting his films. How else can one explain that his movie, *Shakespeare in Love*, beat out *Saving Private Ryan* for Best Picture in 1998?

All evidence would indicate that this *quid pro quo* is nothing new in the movie industry (and, sadly, it is also alive and well in many other endeavors). The casting couch in the movie industry has accommodated two people almost since the motion picture medium was invented. Rather than expressing that they are "shocked, *shocked*!" by these revelations, perhaps Hollywood insiders should admit that the culture of tolerating bad behavior by successful movie moguls has existed for some time.

The American motion picture industry is a culture where a few people, mostly men, hold positions of power. The aspirants know that the difference between waiting on tables and riding a limousine is getting that big break. Many of these aspiring actors are young and are blessed by heredity with extraordinary beauty. What could possibly go wrong?

When anyone achieves a position of power on a large scale, sustained by a record of success, opportunities for bad behavior abound. Success can truly hide many sins of leaders at the top. Industry insiders knew for decades about the slimy behavior of Harvey Weinstein.[24] But he knew how to spot and develop winning films and plays, probably better than anyone else in the industry. In addition to being feted and lauded within his industry and by various American politicians, Harvey Weinstein was also made an honorary Commander of the Order of the British Empire and a knight of the Legion of Honor of France. Although people are now queuing up to register their condemnation of Harvey Weinstein, in Academy Awards acceptance speeches throughout the past fifty years, Harvey Weinstein has been thanked by award recipients as often as winners have thanked God (thirty-four times).[25] All of us, even when we enjoy the luxury of free choice, respect power and success, and most of us will endure an incredible amount of abuse from a superior to bask in the bright light of power.

---

[24] As host of the Oscars in February 2013, Seth MacFarlane said of the nominees for Best Supporting Actress, "Congratulations. You five ladies no longer have to pretend to be attracted to Harvey Weinstein."

[25] The count of "thanks" at the Oscars seems to be hard to pin down, but I obtained this information from: Rodriguez, Ashley. "How Powerful Was Harvey Weinstein? Almost No One Has Been Thanked at the Oscars More." *Quartz*. October 14, 2017. https://qz.com/1101213/harvey-weinstein-is-one-of-the-most-thanked-people-in-oscars-history/.
Ziv, Stav. "At Oscars, Harvey Weinstein Thanked More than God, According to 2015 Analysis." *Newsweek*, October 10, 2017. https://www.newsweek.com/oscars-harvey-weinstein-thanked-more-god-according-2015-analysis-681593. Ziv gives a slightly different number than Rodriguez, but the point remains the same—Harvey Weinstein was a successful movie producer and a terrible leader.

The culture of Hollywood, laid bare by the Weinstein scandal, is merely an exaggerated (and glitzy) version of where human nature will often go. Success not only clouds the judgment of people looking on from the outside (Weinstein's behavior was an open secret in Hollywood), but success also distorts the judgment of the *followers* of successful tyrants. Let us look at a very dangerous job that never lacked for applicants.

Subordinates As Enablers Of Bad Leadership: Oh, So You Want To Be The Grand Vizier?

Being the grand vizier, or first minister, of the Ottoman Empire (1200–1918) was a risky job. A modern job posting for the position would read something like this:

- Benefits
    - You will be the second-most-powerful man in this multi-cultural empire that extends into three continents.

    - Your boss, the sultan, has absolute power, and that power flows down to you; you'll be the center of many large ceremonies, and you will never lack for sycophants.

    - If you have a good relationship with the sultan, your daughter might become one of his many wives.

- Challenges
    - Your boss, the sultan, has absolute power. He can behave in any manner he chooses. If he gets angry, he may kill you.

    - If you fail in a grand enterprise, this will really make the sultan mad; see the above bullet.

    - The Empire can be a violent place; during rebellions, mobs may kill you.

During the seven centuries of that huge empire's existence, over 15 percent of grand viziers were executed by their boss, the sultan. One sultan, aptly named Selim the Grim, executed seven grand viziers, and yet there was never a shortage of men willing to step up to assume the role. The lure of power is strong, and people will take many chances to be close to it. The greater the scale and scope of the organization, the greater the power at the pinnacle, and the greater the attraction to it. Leaders at the top know this. While some leaders refrain from taking advantage of their power, too many others delight in their ability to bask in and abuse it. As long as they are perceived to be successful, these poor leaders will remain practitioners of Leadership Lite; leadership without the element of character.

The Challenge Of Leadership Lite

The examples of Harvey Weinstein and other high-level bad leaders introduced a serious challenge to my idealized model of leadership, especially one that emphasized the importance of character. Did the actions of Weinstein, my character-deficient archetype, achieve the organizational goals? Yes. He led the production of highly successful movies and plays. Did he get discretionary effort from the people he led? That is a more difficult question to answer because Weinstein was a producer, not a director. In most cases, he was not involved in the day-to-day activities of creating films. But he certainly possessed the ability, as a producer, to select projects and to assemble the resources to undertake them. What was it like for the people who worked directly for him in his company?

A recent *Los Angeles Times* article suggested that Harvey Weinstein achieved his success in the manner of most tyrants—he cycled people through his self-generated meat grinder, driven by bullying.[26] Ambitious people were eager to run the gauntlet for a year or so to work in his company to gain experience, which could then be parlayed into better jobs in other companies. As one former employee put it, "The company was packed full of young people, driven by the idea that they were cheap. The attitude was that the company paid them with experience. The abusive behavior was part of the deal." Another observer noted, "You put in your year or two, then you got the hell out of there."[27]

---

[26] Ng, David, Ryan Faughnder, and Andrea Chang. "Working for Harvey Weinstein Was a Coveted Career Steppingstone That Came at a Price." *Los Angeles Times*. October 14, 2017. https://www.latimes.com/business/hollywood/la-fi-ct-weinstein-employees-20171014-story.html.
[27] Ibid.

Did Harvey Weinstein get that extra effort, that discretionary effort, from his subordinates? Overall, the answer appears to be no, not in the long term. Most people simply couldn't hang around him for very long. And even before the stories of his sexual harassment emerged, his company was starting to falter, with departures of key executives and falling revenues. Now that his name is poison in the industry he so recently dominated, there will probably be very little left as an institutional legacy of his work. Even in the wink-wink, nod-nod culture of Hollywood, character finally arose as a critical factor in leadership, bringing down a tyrant after far too many years. (I also predict that similar scandals will continue to emerge in several organizations for many years to come—stay tuned.)

The Secrets Of Leadership Lite

It is abundantly clear from history and recent headlines that people with serious character deficiencies can reach high positions of leadership. How do they do it, and why do we tolerate it? Probably the truism most painful for an idealist to stomach is that noble intent, by itself, is never a guarantee of success. A leader can be extraordinarily effective in giving direction and displaying the capabilities to direct resources to achieve success, sometimes at an incredible level. With that success, the leader accrues more and more power, even though character may be lacking.

The great British historian, Lord Acton, is famous for his aphorism about power and corruption, but let us examine the larger context of his famous quotation from an April 1887 letter to the Bishop of London, Mandell Creighton:[28]

> "Power tends to corrupt and absolute power corrupts absolutely. Great men are almost always bad men, even when they exercise influence and not authority; still more when you superadd the tendency of the certainty of corruption by authority."

As long as we humans intend to live beyond the scale of hunter/gatherers, we will have hierarchies, for only through hierarchies can we

---

[28] Lord Acton's full name was John Emerich Edward Dalberg-Acton, first Baron Acton: historian, English-German, Catholic (at a time when Catholics were discriminated against for public office in the UK), Liberal Party MP. In his lectures of modern history, given in 1895, he said of Oliver Cromwell, "There is not a more perilous or immoral habit of mind than the sanctifying of success."

achieve anything in scale. Therefore, despite Lord Acton's warning, we will still require "great" men and women to lead us at those levels. Both history and today's news are replete with examples of "bad," and "corrupt" leaders who have risen through Leadership Lite—they have either been incredibly lucky (e.g., heredity) or were able to provide direction and demonstrate the capabilities necessary for their organization to succeed, sometimes with spectacular results, despite a lack of character.

I faced this dilemma: I knew that my three elements were the essence of effective leadership, but did not coalesce as often as they should, especially at the higher levels of a hierarchy, where subordinates will tolerate a lot of abuse, and the top leader's image and character can be faked. To offer a basic model to help develop *capable* leaders of character, I now had to modify my model.

CHAPTER 7

My Leadership Model: Revised With Help From Attila The Hun

THE PREVAILING POPULAR VIEW: *"If your intentions are good and if you really want to make a difference, you'll succeed as a leader."*

TOUGH LOVE REALITY: *Good intentions alone will never guarantee success as a leader. The impact of character is dependent on a foundation of competence. Hard work and skill are required.*

I had begun to address this dilemma about leadership—how could so many people who were clearly not good leaders still survive and even prosper? My answer, which I should have developed sooner, was based on my own experience: Success can hide many sins, especially in the short run. Leaders who were highly capable in giving direction and demonstrating a high level of capabilities could achieve success, and the glow of that success could mask deficiencies in character.

While Leadership Lite has often been judged *successful* (once again, most often in the short run), it wasn't *capable* leadership, let alone *inspiring* leadership. Leadership Lite leaves followers fearful, not inspired. Capable leadership is cumulative in its effects, bringing imitation, and that imitation benefits the *organization* over time, transcending the individual leader. Leadership Lite seldom benefits long-term organizational health.

It certainly can generate significant wealth, but the main focus and beneficiary of Leadership Lite is the leader him- or herself. "It's all about me" is the motto of Leadership Lite.

As we have seen, the practitioner of Leadership Lite can be so visibly successful that he or she can attract subordinates with the allure of power, then replace them at a brutal rate, obviating the need for character and the discretionary effort from followers. This approach turns the old saw about making lemonade from lemons on its head: You treat people like lemons, squeeze them for juice, and then throw them away. One of the most salient features of Leadership Lite is that the leader seldom orchestrates a successful succession; things collapse once he or she is gone.

A great example of this is none other than the "Scourge of God" himself, Attila the Hun. As the leader of the Huns, a tribe of nomads from the Eurasian steppes, Attila cobbled together an army of various tribes during the fifth century AD, as the western half of the Roman Empire was collapsing. His army was predatory in the extreme, attacking and destroying cities across Europe, using terror to discourage resistance. Records are scarce regarding Attila's ethnic origins and appearance, but records from the places he attacked in his twenty-year career as king of the Huns provide ample evidence of his terrible effectiveness. It clearly required a dominant personality to hold this disparate army of plunderers together, but upon Attila's death, his empire completely and rapidly collapsed. Lack of continuity is a common theme where leadership is excessively dependent on the one person at the top. However, Attila's reputation has survived in colorful ways; after the release of the movie *Paint Your Wagon*, a box-office bomb in 1969, the director, Joshua Logan, said of his difficult star, "Not since Attila the Hun swept across Europe leaving 500 years of total darkness has there been a man like Lee Marvin."

How then, do we encourage leadership, with all its elements, to avoid developing or encouraging future Attila-the-Hun imitators? To achieve cumulative improvement (the betterment of the human condition over time), organizational cohesion must be maintained beyond the leadership of one personality. Direction, capabilities, and character remain the key elements for leadership, but interactions and dependencies among these elements are more complex than a simple Venn diagram. A different diagram emerged in my model: a diagram that conveys that these elements interact and build upon each other:

Character - HOW

Capabilities - WHAT

Direction - WHY

Direction

> "It is not enough to do your best; you must know what to do, and then do your best."
> – W. Edwards Deming

The first element, direction, is now the foundation stone of the revised model. The leader must envision and communicate the purpose, the *Why* of the endeavor. Without a well-stated direction, energy will be wasted, and frustration will fester, despite the leader's abilities in the other two elements, capabilities and character. Within the context of large organizations, a leader at any level must first discern and conform to the direction of higher echelons. In small organizations, especially start-ups, the most important aspect of direction is to focus on what needs to be done, which also addresses the all-important flip-side of that question—what are we *not* going to do?

Capabilities: Actions To Match Words

In demonstrating capabilities, the leader shows what sets him or her apart—why he or she *deserves* to be a leader at that level. This does not mean that the leader must excel at every job in the organization; our enterprises are far too complex, and change is too rapid to expect that level of performance. But followers rightfully expect a leader to be competent at the level at which he or she is operating (and in most cases, being paid). This is why, for capabilities, scale *does* matter. At whatever level a leader operates, she or he must be competent managing at that level.

The third element, character (the most important for pure leadership) rests on the first two elements.

The Problem With Character

The challenges that accompany the third model element, character, are best addressed by this model of a "build;" that is, showing that the impact of character is dependent on the first two elements. This brings us to the most important challenge of this book:

Good intentions alone will never guarantee successful leadership.

This suggests an even more discouraging corollary—reliance on good intentions alone will almost always guarantee failure. People do not rally to follow repeated failures, no matter how noble the cause.

Character is the most important element for producing outstanding leadership because outstanding leadership generates discretionary effort in followers, which leads to cumulative improvement. But character's effectiveness in leadership is dependent on a foundation of direction and capabilities.

The "Best Leader" Exercise

A common practice in leadership discussions is to ask participants to identify an outstanding leader from their own experience, someone for whom they worked who conveyed the best aspects of leadership to inspire them—their *best leader*. I have led this exercise in many different venues for many different companies over the past thirty years. Over time, I have learned to set a few parameters in order to establish a good baseline for comparisons. For example, I do not allow participants to use a family member as their *best leader* example, because I have observed that family relationships can encompass unique

> **Good intentions alone will never guarantee successful leadership.**

aspects that don't apply outside the family. Would the leadership behavior of that eccentric uncle or aunt *really* work outside the context of the family? But with this constraint in place, some important, consistent themes have emerged.

First, examples people have offered have seldom been someone remote. The examples are always an immediate boss and describe a direct interaction with that leader. In my experience with this exercise, people have never named a United States president giving a speech; neither have I ever heard of a CEO visit as an example of a *best leader*.

Second, the leader's interaction is invariably quite personal, and it often involves the leader showing concern or confidence regarding the follower. Sometimes the example is a teacher who pulled the student aside and encouraged her or him, not in a general manner but in a very specific way, unique to that individual. Other examples include supervisors who toiled under difficult work conditions with followers (out in the rain and the mud instead of staying in a warm hut) or a boss who gave followers a stretch assignment but also gave them guidance to succeed.

In these discussions, I ask the question, "Did this leader inspire you to do more?" and the responses have consistently been a definite *yes*. From these examples and my own experiences, I have come to appreciate the power of effective leadership to inspire that extra, or discretionary, effort from followers. But it is also critical to see where, within the organization, that inspiration occurs. Nearly all examples come from within the immediate group, from that close, inner circle of personal relationships reflected by Dunbar's Number. Since the outstanding leader exercise is about identifying the leadership you want to emulate, this reinforces the concept: Probably the most effective and important leadership is practiced at the direct, personal level because this is the level where the leader's character is revealed in its most authentic form.

But perhaps the most important insight I have gained conducting these exercises is this confirmation: giving direction and displaying capabilities are the foundation upon which character must rest. When I ask each person if that leader was capable in his or her job, the answers have been remarkably consistent—*absolutely*. In hearing these examples, I started to realize that good and noble intentions, by themselves, are not sufficient for leadership effectiveness. The leader has to be effective in giving direction, and the leader has to gain credibility by showing capabilities in his or her job *before* followers experience the full impact of character. Direction and capabilities are the table stakes for character, and they do not require years of observation. Followers can assess them fairly quickly within the small group, and reputation can certainly play a role to instill confidence rapidly with followers.

But these observations suggest a harsh reality. No matter how much we may want to succeed, no matter how pure our intentions may be, we still need *first* to be competent at our jobs to be effective leaders. In fast-moving situations, where both the scope of our jobs (internal forces) and the external context or environment of our efforts can change suddenly and often, the odds of getting in over one's head in a job have increased. During one presentation, a participant privately confided in me that he once found himself promoted to a level that greatly exceeded his skill level. His *intentions* were right, but he soon realized he lacked the level of competence that the job required to be an effective leader. After that conversation, I reviewed my own experiences, and I found at least one situation where I was also very much in the deep end of the pool and sinking, and good intentions provided no buoyancy.

Getting the base of direction and capabilities right for a new leadership role is essential for success. In the (rare) organization where role stability and reasonable predictability still exist, the organization has no excuse for placing people in positions far beyond their competence. But since today so many aspects of our work (both internal and external) are so changeable, the individual must take it upon him- or herself to mitigate shortfalls in capabilities when assuming a new role. The obvious advice is not to allow yourself to be thrown into the deep end without swimming lessons. In the worst case, when you are assigned a new role from which you can't back out, and where you are now clearly beyond your current level of skills and knowledge, you must acquire the resources to make up for your shortfall, especially in the short term. In these vulnerable situations, you need capable subordinates whose success is tied closely to your success.

The Enlightened Failure

Each of us has probably observed at least one example of someone with good intentions who failed for lack of knowledge or skill, and history is littered with the corpses of well-intentioned failures. Joseph II (1741–1790), Emperor of Austria, was one of three enlightened despots of his age, in the company of his contemporaries, Frederick II of Prussia (a.k.a. Frederick the Great) and Catherine II of Russia (a.k.a. Catherine the Great). The term *enlightened despot* connotes a near-absolute ruler who wants to use his or her authority to rationalize government and society according to the principles of the Enlightenment, which means applying scientific (as opposed to traditional, customary, or religious) principles to government, as well as applying a humane approach to society. The term *enlightened* should not be taken too literally using today's standards; these rulers were not proto-democrats in any sense. They thoroughly believed in their divine right to rule as monarchs. While rationalizing government processes often *did* involve bettering the lives of peasants (by improving productivity and encouraging commerce), the main advantages gained by these despots' efforts were more efficient tax collection, better armies, and reducing the power of landed nobles (history's exemplars of unruly subordinates).

Joseph II assumed the throne in 1780 and immediately set out to impose changes based on enlightened thinking. His changes involved fairer taxation, health improvements, education, and religious tolerance, to name only a few. From the vantage point of over 200 years later, his efforts appear genuinely enlightened. But he failed as a leader to make his changes enduring, because he failed to establish a base that would accept and promulgate these changes. Possessing too great a belief in the power of his own authority, he tried to accomplish too much in too short a time, and he proceeded to alienate almost every segment of society that was necessary to support him and his ideas, including his inner circle. He also wasted efforts becoming involved in too many details. For example, the story that Mozart (who died in Vienna in 1791) was buried in a pauper's grave is incorrect. Mozart was buried in a common grave in the outskirts of Vienna because the recently deceased Joseph II had established a law requiring common burials for *most* of his subjects, a rational approach to problems like public health.

Joseph II had many good intentions, and his efforts were truly admirable. But he neglected a key part of the program: getting it done. Joseph made the fatal error of thinking that good ideas succeed simply by being good ideas. He decreed that Latin would no longer be the official language of government, replacing it with German. This decree was based on solid rational principles, but it did not go down well with Hungarian nobles, a key non-German speaking group within his empire. This pattern occurred with almost each of Joseph II's efforts: a great idea which immediately alienated a key constituency and therefore doomed its success. Joseph also failed in the area where success was the most obvious and celebrated in that age: war. While his contemporaries, Frederick and Catherine, won many victories and expanded their territory, Joseph's military efforts expended much treasure without results. Note that both Frederick and Catherine, who were probably more cynical and less enlightened than Joseph, are today labeled "Great," while Joseph, who appears to have been genuinely decent, is not. Sadly, Joseph asked that his epitaph read, "Here lies Joseph II, who failed in all he undertook."

As we will explore in the final section of this book, while leadership at the top of large-scale endeavors may give the *appearance* of total control, the reality is more often dependence on organizationally loyal, competent followers, especially effective subordinate *leaders*. In societies with some measure of free choice, ruling by decree alone seldom works, especially for effecting rapid change.

Even in organizations of large scale, the close-in leadership with immediate subordinates is often the most crucial leadership relationship for success for the leader at the top. Even with digitization (see Chapter

11), efforts are still filtered through layers of human beings in execution, especially those undertakings that require a change in behavior.

In the pantheon of ineffective leadership, a derivative of the enlightened failure is the panderer to popularity. This leader has no real plan, individual mission, or values, but shifts in the wind, responding to whatever whims emerge from his or her followers. This weak leader believes that making connections with followers is the end-in-itself for leadership, forgetting that leaders are given their role for a purpose—to lead those followers to achieve the organizational goals. The panderers' standards and values are usually quite elastic, which results in a leadership vacuum. This leadership weakness is often seen in over-indulgent parents and in "easy" teachers.

My Taxonomy Of Leadership

The goal of any leadership development program should be to identify, develop, and promote leaders who demonstrate all three elements: direction, capabilities, and character. Within the circle of a leader's close relationships (where the leader cannot hide any flaws), *pure leadership*— the fundamental form of leadership—is practiced. No matter the level of the leader within the organization, all leaders will exercise this leadership with their core group. When these leaders employ all three elements effectively, they are *capable leaders*, and they are needed at every level of every group or organization. When the conditions demand it, the best of these leaders can rise to be *inspiring leaders*.

Less robust forms of leadership certainly exist, and not all forms are harmful. A talented specialist can exercise *indirect leadership* through reputation, which is a diluted form of leadership, that is, leadership without formal authority. In my experience, this form of leadership requires significant time to develop, and it seldom successfully transitions into a position of formal authority over a large group of followers.

Regrettably, some forms of bad leadership are alive and well. Leadership Lite is the successful exercise of direction and capabilities without necessary character. But there is another form of bad leadership, similarly well-developed in higher positions in large hierarchies: rent-seeking leaders who inhabit the Executive Bubble, drifting along, putting as much distance between them and their followers as they can. They are the focus of the next chapter.

CHAPTER 8

Beware Of The Executive Bubble: The Realm Of The Rent-Seeking Leader

THE PREVAILING POPULAR VIEW: *"Executives can see the big picture at their level, and then jump in."*

TOUGH LOVE REALITY: *Some executives can use their position to conveniently distance themselves from the core work of the organization. They orbit a different sun.*

After Leadership Lite and the well-intentioned failure, the *Executive Bubble* is the next threat to effective leadership at the highest levels of an organization. While Leadership Lite uses success to mask deficiencies in character, the Executive Bubble uses the status of the position to avoid leadership duties. The Executive Bubble creates the reverse of the problem Moses faced: While Moses was overwhelmed by the demands of his followers, occupants of the Executive Bubble intentionally remove themselves from the demands of their followers.

To explore this, first let me explain my basic taxonomy of positions in the hierarchy of large organizations:

- The **supervisor** leads his or her group directly and operates in a specific skill area.

- The **manager** leads supervisors directly, operating in a common skill area.

- The **general manager** (sometimes called a **director**) leads managers and operates across a wide spectrum of skill areas.

- The **executive** operates at the highest levels of the organization, leading units across the organization and influencing outside entities (investors, the press, government bodies, etc.) as well.

Specialists also occupy many positions throughout the organization, including executive roles such as general counsel. The value of these executives is mostly their specialist skills, not their leadership skills, and they expend most of their effort within their specialty, not leading. My focus in this discussion, however, is on the executives who have *leadership* roles in organizational operations, who must direct general managers, staff, and others in core functions of the enterprise.

As in so many of our interactions with one another, any leader must achieve a delicate balance regarding how deeply to intervene in the workings of the organization. As Moses discovered with the help of Jethro, we're limited in how much we can take on as an individual, which is why hierarchy is necessary. But there is also a risk of becoming *too* removed from the work of the organization (and thereby too removed from the people you're leading). Distance can erode a leader's effectiveness. The healthcare industry in the United States provides an illustration of this problem. Significant consolidation is happening across the United States; small, stand-alone hospitals are being acquired by much larger hospital systems.

To explore the risk, I am taking my own experiences in so-called mergers, and applying them in the example of healthcare throughout the country, as small hospitals are acquired by larger corporations, to show, in a composite example, how the Executive Bubble could impact the nursing staff.

Small Regional Hospital

Throughout the United States, larger hospital systems are taking over smaller, formerly independent hospitals. In this particular example, Small Community Hospital (SCH) was acquired by Big City Hospital System (BCHS). Small Community Hospital had the usual challenges of small hospitals, such as limited financial resources, limited in-house resources, and limited educational support for staff, but this hospital had established a very effective culture among its nurses over many years. The nursing staff had developed capable processes leading to continuous improvement, had maintained good morale, and had won numerous national awards, which resulted in excellent patient safety and patient/employee satisfaction scores.

Due to our penchant to focus on status, nurses occupy a profession that is often overlooked in importance when compared to physicians, but we should all remember that the last person we will see before we leave this earth will probably be a nurse.

In many respects, the *smaller* scale of this community hospital had aided the development of this excellent culture in its nursing division. The "universe" for leaders in this hospital was, simply, only this one hospital. Continuity and longevity in jobs meant that leaders could not only track progress over time, but also that participants *owned* the processes. Within the nursing division (the largest group of employees in the hospital), programs of improvement really worked, and the buy-in and participation were genuine throughout the ranks. The discretionary effort was alive and well. The culture kept standards high; new nurses quickly adopted the standards or they left. Most nurses enjoyed working in such a competent environment, and turnover was low. Because of the limited scale of SCH (and therefore, a more limited division of labor compared to huge hospital systems), its nursing leaders had to possess a wide range of knowledge and experience to manage all the moving parts of the organization and to maintain its highly effective culture.

Big City Hospital System

The overriding reality of the business model driving consolidation of individual hospitals into larger healthcare systems throughout the United States is the financial weakness of operating on a small scale. In this case, BCHS acquired SCH. Such transactions are *always* acquisitions, never mergers.

BCHS certainly had tremendous advantages of scale, which would help with the business model going forward. But the culture in nursing throughout BCHS was not nearly as effective as that at SCH. None of the many BCHS hospitals could match the record of SCH in nursing. SCH was poised to provide BCHS the methods it had used to achieve its nursing accomplishments. You would think this would have been an ideal situation: spread SCH's best practices throughout the BCHS. But in fact, the exact opposite occurred. BCHS overlooked this opportunity, and the culture of SCH nurses deteriorated as a result. I believe the major factor in this unfortunate turn of events was the Executive Bubble.

Operating In A Separate World

Upon taking control of SCH, the BCHS executives established the overriding importance of corporate control—centralized decisions from system headquarters. While there were certainly some areas where this approach was appropriate (achieving economies of scale in purchasing supplies and equipment, for example), this sweeping effect (the corporate mothership knows best) quickly eroded the culture of improvement that had been painstakingly developed in nursing over decades at SCH. BCHS executives were unfamiliar with the effort required to maintain a culture of improvement within the SCH, and they didn't realize that a community hospital was different from the other hospitals in their system. The new executives and general managers from the BCHS filling the top nursing positions were not only utterly disinterested in what SCH nurses had accomplished over time; they were also sublimely indifferent to many of the immediate issues at SCH. The root of the problem was that BCHS leaders' *orientation* was completely different.

The newly arrived BCHS executives were part of a large, closed group of executives who moved frequently from one position to another, from one hospital to another within the BCHS. Their world was not the place where they had their office or the people they led; it was the executive group within which they moved. It was their movement within the Executive Bubble that mattered, not their commitment to a specific job (out of which they would rotate quickly, anyway). In SCH's previous culture, nursing executives, general managers, and managers had been expected to know their jobs in breadth (not only clinical aspects but also supply, pharmacy, etc.) and in detail (how process improvement efforts were proceeding, who needed updated certification, and so forth). BCHS executives expected to be completely shielded from these "mundane" issues, and this habit extended down to new general managers as well. Almost their entire attention was directed to internal maneuverings within the Executive Bubble—who reports to whom, internal reports within the Bubble, what's the next career move, and so forth.

When SCH was a stand-alone entity, some general managers wore scrubs as often as they wore suits so they could jump in to help in a pinch. Leaders knew everyone in their departments, and leaders were visible. Under the new regime, executives and general managers became much less visible. Offices became off-limits to walk-ins. And new high-level leaders often didn't bother to learn employees' names. The impact on the organization, however, was more insidious than mere hurt feelings. Nurses and other staff members began to keep their heads down and "stay in their lane" rather than giving any extra effort.

Did this hospital break down? No. Large organizations maintain considerable momentum, and this hospital continues to function. But morale among nursing staff has deteriorated, and the carefully developed culture of continuous improvement has been weakened. Will this impact patient care? Possibly, since a general correlation between hospital employee satisfaction and patient care seems to exist, and this type of adverse trend could affect all of us, as potential patients.[29]

---

[29] Walker, Angelina. "Nursing Satisfaction Impacts Patient Outcomes, Mortality." Nurse.org. Accessed March 12, 2019. https://nurse.org/articles/nursing-satisfaction-patient-results/.

The Executive Rent-Seeker

This consolidated example shows one of the all-too-frequent downsides of big organizational scale. Among new executives and general managers from BCHS, their position in the hierarchy had become an end in itself, not a means to an end.

Executives who occupy their position only for their own individual benefit are the leadership equivalents of rent-seekers.

In economics, rent-seeking is the use of economic resources or position to achieve a financial gain without the creation of wealth. Examples are policy manipulation, bribery, or monopolistic control—in essence, manipulation without productivity. This approach is the bane of true economic progress since no one benefits except the rent-seeker. This analogy holds for the executive (or anyone in a position of authority) who occupies a position only for his or her own benefit. Self-interest will always be a factor in our actions, but it should never be the *only* factor. Large organizations are especially vulnerable to the Executive Bubble, because they have the scale to create it. Within that separate world, the pursuit of self-interest can be raised to an art form. While focusing upward or horizontally within the Executive Bubble, a leader is less prone to dedicate her or his capabilities to solving problems with followers to make things better.

> Executives who occupy their position only for their own individual benefit are the leadership equivalents of rent-seekers.

Capable leaders at the top levels *should* want to know about issues throughout their organization so they can prioritize and address them, and then use their ability to manage resources to improve the work being performed. Of course, they need subordinates to help filter and arrange the problems, but no executive should use his or her position to avoid knowing what's going on.

To reiterate, at the executive level, the leader doesn't have to be the absolute best leader in the entire organization, but he or she *must* be a capable leader. We must resist the natural inclination to orient upward to the neglect of our followers; rather, we must demonstrate to them why we were elevated to a leadership position in the first place.

In economics, the prosperity of nations is achieved by the generation of wealth, not its hoarding or manipulation. In leadership, using a position to avoid responsibility should raise the question: Why does that person occupy that position in the first place? Rent-seeking leadership generates no discretionary effort, no cumulative improvement.

Where Bad Leadership Further Devolves

Both the leader deficient in character (Leadership Lite) and the rent-seeking, responsibility-avoiding leader can easily deteriorate further into the epitome of bad leadership: *the corrupt leader*. I define corruption in the classic sense: *the use of a leadership role to enrich the leader, to the detriment of the common effort*. Corruption is corrosive to the fiber of organizations and society because it subverts the purpose of leadership—to achieve organizational goals. The temptations for leader enrichment are many:

- Probably the most common form of corruption is a monetary reward beyond what is due as payment for service. Studies have demonstrated that we have no limit to what we think we are worth, or what we think we deserve, so the temptation to use a position of leadership for personal gain will always be present. This explains why the occasional executive earning seven figures continues to cheat for petty amounts of money on expense reports.

- Leaders at the top can also be tempted to use the status of position to gain personal gratification. Harvey Weinstein illustrates the widespread use of position by men in power to employ the workplace as a dating pool, now coming more prominently to light. But, sadly, this is nothing new: The Old Testament relates the story of King David sending Uriah the Hittite to certain death in the Israelite army so that David could enjoy Uriah's wife, Bathsheba.

- Finally, leaders can misuse their positions of power by focusing the entire endeavor on themselves, where *they* become the end-in-itself. From vast vanity projects to attaching the leader's name to any successful outcome (irrespective of any real cause-and-effect relationship), these actions show the forceful transforming of the common effort into a cult of the personality. As the psychopathic Roman emperor, Nero, died, his last words lamented how the world was losing such an artist. Another frustrated artist and psychopath nearly two thousand years later, who visited far more destruction on the world in the name of his own vanity, lamented at the end of his life how the German people were unworthy of him—Adolf Hitler. These are extreme examples, but they dramatically illustrate the inclination to abuse power in leadership positions to stoke one's oversized ego.

But one rare leadership phenomenon makes leading appear effortless: the *charismatic leader.* This is the leader who seems to gather and direct a loyal following with perfect ease. This is also the most dangerous type of leadership.

CHAPTER 9

Charisma: The Deadly Shortcut

The prevailing popular view: *"Charisma is highly desirable and can be taught."*

TOUGH LOVE REALITY: *Charisma is the rare ability to have followers suspend their judgment and follow without hesitation; in nearly all cases, charisma is dangerous.*

lutarch was a Greek who wrote in the first century AD during the full brilliance of the Roman Empire, and his most famous work is his *Lives*, or more precisely, *The Lives of the Noble Grecians and Romans.*[30] In this work, Plutarch examined the biographies of famous Greeks and Romans, paying particular attention to their character. Until about 100 years ago, this book was required reading for members of the educated, elite class in the West. *Plutarch's Lives* was one of the key sources for the Founding Fathers of the United States; it was also a source of insight for Harry Truman, our last president who did not hold a college degree (he couldn't afford to complete college), but who nonetheless was a remarkably wise man.

> "They just don't come better than old Plutarch."
> —HARRY TRUMAN

---

[30] The story of Alcibiades and the quotations are taken from Plutarch, John Dryden, and Arthur Hugh Clough. *Plutarch: The Lives of the Noble Grecians and Romans.* New York: Modern Library, 1992.

One of the most instructive lives related by Plutarch is that of Alcibiades of Athens, who lived from about 450 BC to 404 BC. For Athens, this period was both splendid (the time of Pericles and Socrates) and turbulent (the Peloponnesian War and plague), and Alcibiades, a flamboyant statesman and general, was a major force in these events. Plutarch tells us that Alcibiades possessed "a grace and a charm." He was strikingly handsome and could persuade people very effectively, especially in one-on-one conversation.

I believe his gift of persuasion suggests that Alcibiades had *charisma*, the ability to secure instant compliance with one's wishes, without having to demonstrate the essential leadership elements of direction, capabilities, and character.

Alcibiades: Brilliant, Unscrupulous, Extravagant

Unfortunately for Athens, there was a dark side to Alcibiades's character: He was utterly self-absorbed. He lived in splendor and flaunted his wealth and power. He was a notorious womanizer. He acted arbitrarily, playing cruel tricks on people and exhibiting a nasty temper. Alcibiades's traits and behavior would have been mere fodder for gossip had he only thrown wild parties during his life, but he involved himself in politics and war, and in these endeavors, his influence was ultimately malevolent.

To describe his complex career very briefly: during the Peloponnesian War against Sparta, Alcibiades convinced Athens to embark on the invasion of Sicily. This campaign was a complete military disaster and a major factor in the ultimate defeat of Athens in the war. Alcibiades later conspired with the Spartans (the enemy of Athens) and even conspired with the Persians, who threatened all of Greece. He seemed to jump back and forth to gain advantage from whomever he could at any given moment. Incredibly, Athens *received him back into politics* after his treacherous liaisons with the Spartans and Persians, but his life ultimately ended badly. At the age of about forty-five, he was assassinated. According to Plutarch the accounts differ: either Alcibiades was killed by political rivals or by brothers who wanted to avenge his rape of their sister.

Despite his obvious character defects, Alcibiades certainly possessed exceptional abilities. He was brave in battle and had led both Athenian naval and land forces to victories earlier in his career. Plutarch quoted the playwright Aristophanes to describe the ambiguous feeling of the people of Athens toward Alcibiades: "They love, and hate, and cannot do without him."[31] His admirers always found ingenious ways to excuse Alcibiades's bad behavior, and he continued to convince Athenians to approve of and support his schemes, all of which eventually ended badly.

The Lesson From 2,400 Years Ago: Beware Of Charisma

Alcibiades is not only an excellent historical example of the dangers of charisma; his Greek origins also convey the original meaning of the word itself, which is Greek for *gift* or *favor*. Although today some leadership practitioners advocate *teaching* charisma, I disagree completely with that approach. I conclude, from the examples from history, that charisma is an inherent trait (or more likely a combination of inherent traits) that causes a specific response from followers:

Charisma causes followers to suspend their careful judgment of a leader—to follow that leader without hesitation.

Research indicates that our brains may suspend their rational processing capabilities under the influence of a charismatic leader: Our brains short-circuit to *yes*.[32] I believe there are two primary causes of this phenomenon: the inherent abilities of a very small group of people who possess charisma, and the receptivity of a particular audience. I maintain that charisma is very rare—that most of us, most of the time, will both lead and follow absent the presence of a charismatic leader. But the existence of charismatic leaders, however rare, is a definite fact of history.

My challenge regarding charisma is that I suggest that in most cases, charisma is a very dangerous phenomenon. We should avoid letting ourselves become ensnared by it. I also maintain that most leaders, even the great leaders of history, have actually *rarely* exuded charisma. Most

---

[31] Ibid., p. 243

[32] Erez, Amir, Vilmos F. Misangyi, Diane E. Johnson, Marcie A. Lepine, and Kent C. Halverson. "Stirring the Hearts of Followers: Charismatic Leadership as the Transferal of Affect." *Journal of Applied Psychology* 93, no. 3 (2008): 602–16. https://doi.org/10.1037/0021-9010.93.3.602.

have initially built a reputation of success, from which an aura of charisma has then emerged.

Surveying the presidents of the United States, let us examine the two who are considered the greatest: Abraham Lincoln and George Washington. Remembering to consider their impact *at the time*, rather than looking back with the knowledge of the outcomes, I doubt any argument can be made that Lincoln possessed charisma. He was vilified by a great number of people, not only from the South, but by some who supported the Union cause as well. Even those who worked closely with him were often frustrated and bewildered by his behavior and actions. I ardently believe Lincoln was a great leader, but he exercised his leadership the way most of us must; by building trust over time by giving direction, exhibiting the capabilities demanded of his position, and showing a solid character that binds others through shared values. He spent most of his effort on his inner circle. When these qualities are perceived to generate success, a virtuous cycle continues to grow, fed by inspiration. It was a long, difficult struggle for Lincoln to achieve such success, and he was struck down just at the moment when others began to realize what a great man he was and what he had accomplished.

Right after Lincoln gave his greatest speech, one Union newspaper described his Gettysburg Address (now considered one of the greatest speeches in the English language) as "dishwatery."[33] Many other reviews were also scathing at the time.

Washington's example may come closer to charisma, but I believe his example falls quite short of Alcibiades's level of charisma. Washington's great accomplishment during the Revolutionary War was to hold the army (and, by extension, the concept of an independent United States) together until his adversary, Great Britain, the greatest military power in the world at that time, gave up. It was a long, difficult, and often thankless task. Sometimes other American generals were maneuvering to take over Washington's command, and one of Washington's subordinates,

---

[33] Chicago Tribune. "Editorial: Lincoln at Gettysburg, 150 Years Later." *Chicago Tribune*. September 08, 2018. Accessed February 12, 2019. https://www.chicagotribune.com/opinion/ct-xpm-2013-11-19-ct-lincoln-gettysburg-edit-1119-20131119-story.html.

Benedict Arnold, went over to the other side. The most remarkable aspect of Washington's eventual success was that he never won a decisive, large-scale victory over the British until Yorktown, which was the decisive siege that ended the war. And that success required considerable help from the French army and navy.

Washington always kept his goal, preserving the army (and the new United States) in mind, despite the pettiness of Congress and various schemers who were ostensibly working toward the same goal. I believe his military skills were solid but not exceptional. Washington's character set him apart as a leader; he showed immense fortitude and patience throughout the long struggle. Congress was a deserving target for his scorn, but Washington controlled his anger. Despite the treachery of Benedict Arnold, most of Washington's subordinates were inspired by his example. His demeanor and appearance were great advantages and certainly more effective in inspiring devotion than Lincoln's demeanor and appearance, which were the butt of contemporaneous jokes.

> **Right after Lincoln gave his greatest speech, one Union newspaper described his Gettysburg Address (now considered one of the greatest speeches in the English language) as "dishwatery." Many other reviews were also scathing at the time.**

Ironically, the environment that shows Washington did *not* possess charisma (immediate adoration and compliance) was the political system that he helped bring into being—the United States government. As president of the new republic, Washington was immersed in the process of making decisions that would never please everyone. After all, he helped create a governing system in which power was distributed, both within the federal government and between the federal government and the states. As president, he was subjected to a fair share of scorn; he had plenty of political critics, and he was undoubtedly happy when he retired after his second term, making the magnificent gesture of separating himself from power by giving it up voluntarily. By refusing to accept unlimited power (which only he, with his status as the victorious general and later, as president, might have engineered), but rather by engaging in a system of shared powers, Washington respected the warnings of the ancients: Do not allow a single leader to emerge supreme, no matter how appealing he or she may be.

As Plutarch pointed out in several of his examples, many leaders gain fame and notoriety early in their careers. Some possess the character to avoid becoming self-absorbed; others, like Alcibiades, do not. Washington followed the example of Cincinnatus, the noble Roman who left a position of power to return to his farm.

Charisma—or Chimera?

Just as we erroneously conflate a high organizational position and excellent leadership, we often link effective leadership to personal charisma when something else may really be at work.

First, what we call charisma is often actually the effect of someone's position or reputation. If someone politically powerful (or a famous celebrity) appears before us, by our nature, we are going to pay a significant amount of attention to that presence. We may even try to compose a selfie with that important person in the background, so that we can bask, however briefly, in that person's fame. When a very important person (VIP) enters a room, we respond with attention. It is not that person's incredible persuasive ability that compels us; it is that we *already* know that person is important before he or she utters a word.

Charisma is frequently assigned as a characteristic *after* the fact of success. We must guard against that tendency. We must be able to identify the real presence of charisma because we must be able to guard against the impact of charisma itself, where we let down our guard and follow without hesitation. When following our fellow flawed humans, it is not in our best interest to suspend our judgment and comply simply because our emotions signal us to do so.

Secondly, people who desire power can work diligently to create an aura of charisma. Although gold was plentiful in the Inca Empire, it was not used as a currency. Gold was instead used to enhance the appearance of the ruler, through highly polished crowns and jewelry. The dazzling image of the Inca king, with sunlight reflected from his golden crown and necklaces, created a sense of awe in observers. Spectacular costumes, monuments, parades, and similar pageantry have been employed by rulers to induce awe since civilization began. Powerful images are effective, but, by themselves, they are not the full force of charisma.

We are not immune to the power of images today. While modern technology has been a blessing in improving our standard of living by a quantum leap, it also provides the means to manufacture and enhance a sense of charisma and to reap the benefit of immediate compliance that follows. The efforts of totalitarians during the twentieth century are well known: Nazi spectacles, Mussolini's "enhancements" of Rome (repaving streets to enable military parades through ancient triumphal arches), and the embalming and deification of Mao and Lenin, all with the purpose of creating a sense of awe (and eager obedience) for these respective regimes and their leaders. Compliance without hesitation is the desire of most charismatic leaders and of those tyrannical regimes that try to generate the same effect.

During elections in democracies, emotional manipulation is certainly subtler and lacks totalitarians' sinister purpose, but is still pervasive. Examine recent American election ads that portray opponents in black-and-white tones with discordant music in the background, while narration tries to link the opposing candidate to something bad. The favored candidate is then always shown in color with inspiring music in the background; and don't forget to show the favored candidate with his or her family (especially with children). Marketers of goods knew long before politicians that many decisions are made quickly, driven by emotion. Our politicians are now catching up to the science.

Charisma, real or imagined, bypasses reasoned judgment, and many are trying to create such conditions to influence us, whether they are selling a candidate or a bar of soap. When this effort relates to power—when we are manipulated to view someone as a charismatic leader—our skepticism should rise accordingly.

The Other Side Of The Charismatic Coin

Leaders may actually possess charisma (very rare), may have charisma attributed to them after successes (far more common), or may try to manipulate our emotions to generate the effects of charisma (see: Marketing for Tyrants). But the impact of charisma is equally dependent on the emotional state of the followers, or the audience. What is the most fertile ground for the impact of charisma? People with a sense of dislocation and perceived threats. Both common experience and research support the observation that people who are in, or believe they are facing, an impending threat and who feel vulnerable are the most likely to switch off the "reasoned judgment" or "skeptical" switch in their brains. In those conditions, we lean toward someone offering a solution, and the simpler the solution, the better.

The most fertile ground is when people perceive their world has been disrupted, when they are in crisis. Crises are the moments that call for the best leadership, but the purpose of inspiring leadership should be to engage each person to contribute to the solution. The lure of charisma, by contrast, is its promise of a stress-free solution—*put your complete trust in the leader*—to relieve the followers of any responsibility. Just follow whatever he or she says, and everything will turn out fine.

> "Everything in the world may be endured except continuing prosperity."
> — JOHANN WOLFGANG VON GOETHE

A great paradox of the Industrial Age (only from 1820 to the present) is that, despite its extraordinary comforts and predictability, we seem to suffer from shared collective feelings of dislocation and unease with greater frequency than during the preindustrial age. Perhaps this is because society was more decentralized in the preindustrial age, or perhaps it is because today's media can amplify the meaning of any event through pervasive mass communications. Although we work far less, with significantly less physical strain, than did our agricultural ancestors, we perceive ourselves as frantically busy and endure a lot of self-generated anxiety. The depressing conclusion is that we are as susceptible to being led astray by charismatic leaders as anyone at any time in history.

Personal Observations On Charisma

I believe true charismatic leaders are very rare, and I am highly skeptical of their benefits, possibly resulting from my own experiences. First, to the best of my knowledge, I don't recall surrendering my sense of caution and skepticism in being led. I have certainly been in the presence of outstanding leaders, and I have been inspired by many of them. But I never felt the urge to follow anyone without stopping and thinking about what I was being asked (or told) to do. My life has spanned thirteen presidents; I can recall only two presidents to whom I felt a strong, personal connection, but this connection wasn't hero-worship or unconstrained devotion.

The most inspiring person I have ever seen in person was Nelson Mandela, whose speeches I heard twice, once in South Africa and once in the UK. To my great dismay, however, today I cannot recall what he said. It was his story and personal example that inspired me, so simply being in his presence was amazing, not his words (and, to be fair to him, he was quite old when I heard him speak).

But there is another underlying reason that contributes to my skepticism about charisma. This phenomenon is frequently associated with great religious leaders. I am unqualified to address any examples except those in Christianity. Regrettably, the two-thousand-year history of Christianity provides many examples of charismatic leaders who used the banner of Christianity to incite violence and do harm: from Cola di Rienzo of fourteenth-century Rome to Savonarola of Florence in the fifteenth century (two charismatic leaders in medieval Italy) to the Taiping Rebellion in China in the mid 1800s. This last event was the largest and bloodiest war of that century, led by Hong Xiuquan, who claimed to be the brother of Jesus.

A more recent example of the dangers of charisma is Jim Jones, an American who resettled his followers to Guyana in 1978, where he and over 900 followers shortly thereafter committed mass suicide after they had murdered a visiting United States Congressman. All of these charismatic religious leaders promised much beneficence and eventually delivered enormous suffering. But as many of these leaders were first emerging, they were *popular*, and not just with their immediate followers. Jim Jones had been feted by powerful politicians and was appointed to a position in the city government in San Francisco. Jones was even awarded a humanitarian award from San Francisco's Glide Memorial Church in 1977, one year before he led the murders and mass suicides.[34] Like Alcibiades, Jones could almost effortlessly get many people to suspend their good judgment and go along with his ideas, both followers and high-level endorsers.

But the history of Christianity also offers more positive, less brutal lessons about the siren song of charisma. For a religious founder whose adherents now number the most in the world, and after whom the calendar year is established for most of the world, Jesus must have been a quite charismatic leader, irrespective of one's religious beliefs. But we should note that in the biblical accounts of his resurrection, he did not choose to reappear before a crowd. Rather, he appeared only to a small group and commanded them to go and preach to the entire world. And his followers do not seem to have been very charismatic. The apostles frequently failed in their attempts to win people over; they were chased out of town, imprisoned, beaten, and eventually executed. In its first 300 years, the spread of Christianity was achieved one person at a time, organically. For those of us in the Christian faith, the divinity of Christ should be a hedge *against* charisma. He alone could be charismatic, and for the rest of us, it's hard work.

---

[34] Sward, Susan. "10 Days That Shook S.F." SFGate. *San Francisco Chronicle*, February 9, 2012.
"The Rev. Cecil Williams of Glide Memorial Methodist Church says Jones was able to blind people with his charisma, and the catastrophe that occurred at Jonestown 'opened our eyes. We won't go along today with anyone who will run over poor people.'"

In the past century, a different type of leader has attempted to don the mantle of charisma: nonreligious, except, of course, for their own deification. Immense misery and ruin have been sown by these leaders, claiming that they, and they alone, possessed the answers to our problems. Whether they appealed through tribalism fueled by social Darwinism (the National Socialist German Workers' Party, aka the Nazis) or through forms of tyranny driven by class resentment (the Communists), their approach and results were the same—hijacking emotions on a grand scale to secure power with no hesitation to use brutal force to maintain that power. In these two instances of twentieth century tyranny on a grand scale (the Nazis and Communism), as well as in countless examples of petty tyrants throughout the world, the tendency of an individual or small group to monopolize power, to the extreme detriment of others, is a recurring danger. Charisma short-circuits our healthy skepticism about leaders, and that lapse can place us under a tyrant, as my final story relates.

When I Really Listened: The Warning About Charisma

My concluding story about charisma reinforces my concern about its inherent risks. Besides graduating from the United States Military Academy at West Point, I also enjoyed the privilege of teaching there a few years later in the Department of History. As an instructor, I met a lot of people who worked behind the scenes at West Point whom I would not have met as a cadet. One of those remarkable people was the Librarian of West Point in the early 1980s, Egon Weiss. A senior faculty member took me to meet Egon in the old Library, and it was one of the most illuminating conversations I have ever had.

Egon told me he grew up in Vienna, Austria. In 1938, Hitler (also born in Austria) as the leader of Germany, achieved the merger of Austria into Nazi Germany. Egon was Jewish, and he and his family had no illusions about how bad this turn of events was. As Hitler triumphantly arrived in Vienna to predominantly adoring crowds, Egon told his father that he was going to blend into the crowd at Hitler's speech, because Egon wanted to view this man who was causing his family such misery. Although his father thought this was a bad idea, Egon persisted and ultimately went to listen to Hitler, and then got back to his family, which was desperately preparing to leave Austria—which it did, successfully.

At this point in the story, Egon looked at me intently, with a kind but firm countenance. I understood he was saying to me, "Young man, listen to this because this is important." Despite my rock-headed nature at the time (my early thirties), I got the message, and completely tuned in. Egon said, *"And Hitler was the greatest orator I have ever heard."*

I have never forgotten this story, and it has stayed with me as a warning about the power of charisma. Egon Weiss, who passed away in 2003 at the age of 84, was telling me that evil can be persuasive, that evil can have charisma.

Very few people in history could convince large groups of people to follow them without a record of performance or formal authority. But a small number of people have possessed this power through charisma. When people suspend their judgment in a rush of excitement and simply follow the leader, the result is almost always extraordinarily bad. In practicing our own leadership abilities and in developing the leadership abilities in others, let us *earn* credibility as leaders, not take shortcuts. And as followers, we must never lose our healthy skepticism. In whatever roles we occupy, we must acknowledge that leadership requires significant work. Charisma is rare and most often dangerous.

Fortunately, we live in a time with few real crises, so we should not be desperately seeking a "man on horseback" to save us. But however infrequently they may arise, crises do happen, and leaders must know how to respond. Next, we examine how leaders should act in a crisis, not through shortcuts or deception, but with an understanding of human nature, self-awareness, and skills built through a lot of practice.

CHAPTER 10

When Leadership Matters Most

The prevailing popular view: *"I'm going to be a heroic leader—all the time!"*

TOUGH LOVE REALITY: *Do the day-to-day hard work and become a capable leader, but also be able to identify the rare moment when you must stand out in a crisis.*

After one of my presentations on leadership, I heard a story from one of the participants. She described an administrator who was capable and well respected. One day, however, there was a serious incident in the building (not a fatal shooting, but an act of violence) and the administrator remained hiding under the desk long after the incident was resolved. This administrator eventually had to be reassigned, because any credibility with subordinates in that organization had now been lost. In that one unusual moment, that administrator had lost the capability to lead.

Despite a constant barrage of messages about violence and despite genuine tragedies that do occur, today we live in a mostly safe and predictable environment, especially when compared to human history up to the present day. Most of the leadership we will exercise in our lives will be under conditions of predictability and routine. Capable leaders operate within that context: They give direction, demonstrate capabilities, and display character in a manner that reflects the expectations of a stable environment. Few people want drama introduced where it is not required.

But crises, however infrequent, do occur, and in these rare moments, a leader must deliberately and forcefully seize the moment. In crisis situations, followers earnestly expect interventions from their leaders. When we sense a significant threat, when our world is badly disrupted, we look *up* for guidance. In crisis situations, leaders must embrace the greatest range of responsibilities from their position and accept that the focus on them will be most intense. In cases of physical danger, the leader's first attribute is bravery. Outside of front-line military and other physically dangerous jobs, these instances are rare, but they can occur, and that brief moment can define the leader for the remainder of his or her life. Examples can be spectacular (such as the siege of Malta) or confined (a farm in Kansas), but the need for inspiring leadership in a crisis extends to all levels.

> "Nothing is better known than the Siege of Malta."
> —Voltaire

Voltaire's comment about an event that occurred 200 years before his own era is ironic today since very few people remember the events to which Voltaire refers. The Great Siege of Malta in 1565 is often described by historians as the greatest siege of all time. The setting was the long struggle between Christian Europe and the Ottoman Turks, and the Turks were advancing into the western Mediterranean. They wanted to capture the island of Malta, which the Turks could then use as a stepping-stone to attack Italy. The defense of the island was entrusted to the Knights Hospitaller, a crusading order, whose Grand Master was Jean Parisot de Valette. The stakes were brutally high: in keeping with the grim wartime behavior of the time, neither side could anticipate mercy. During the siege, the Turks would float the mutilated dead bodies of captives toward the fortifications of the Knights, who responded by decapitating their Turkish prisoners and firing the heads out of cannons back at the Turks.

The odds were not in Valette's favor. The Turks landed between 35,000 and 40,000 soldiers on the small island to fight against Valette's force of fewer than 6,000 combatants. But Valette had prepared defenses well, and he accurately anticipated the Turks' moves to take the island. Valette made quick and firm decisions, sometimes acting against the advice of others. Most importantly, when the fighting was most desperate, Valette could be prominently seen among the fighters. Accounts said it was as if he was everywhere, and his presence inspired all defenders. After three months of the siege, the Turks withdrew. Malta was saved, and the Turks never ventured to conquer the western Mediterranean again. The capital city of Malta is Valletta, named in his honor.

From Malta To Kansas?

Malta, of course, is an extreme example, but leaders at any level can derive lessons from Valette. There was no ambiguity about his being in charge. He was visible; he reassured his followers, but he was not naïve or unrealistic. Crucially for a crisis, Valette gave firm direction. When followers in trying situations are given tasks so they can focus on action, as opposed to dwelling on their situation, they respond much better.

Crises can occur on a grand scale, like the Great Siege of Malta, or they can happen to remarkably small groups. On a farm in western Kansas during the Great Depression, a family watched a sudden storm gather and drop hail on the wheat crop that was just ripening before harvest. The entire crop, and therefore the year's income from the crop, was destroyed in a few minutes. The farmer watched from the window of the farmhouse with his wife, daughter, and son. The wife was shattered because the family had not had good harvests for years; this was a terrible disappointment. The daughter was crying because she was in college and didn't know where tuition money was going to come from. The younger son was crushed because he was preparing to start college, and now that didn't seem possible. The farmer said to all of them, "Somehow, it's going to be all right." Then he told each of them what to do in the moment to get everyone engaged.

This was a favorite story of my father's. He recently passed away at the age of ninety-four. He was the son in the narrative. My father never forgot how his own father took on the fears of everyone in the family and guided them forward; how his father did not despair, despite the soul-crushing turn of events. My father related how his father calmly gave them things to do, to take their mind off the deep disappointment, at least for a while; how he led them so they would not give up. And it did turn out all right—weeks later, a distant relative left a modest inheritance that allowed the daughter to continue in college, and the son to enter college. The family held together. Since my father met my mother during that first year in college, I believe I owe my very existence to the calming leadership of my grandfather, for which I will always be grateful.

Step Up—Never Step Away

It is easy to step away from challenging situations if one's position allows for such maneuvering, but that behavior is blatant avoidance of leadership, often aided and abetted by the Executive Bubble. Whether a crisis is externally caused or internally triggered, these are the moments when leadership is immediately needed. If a subordinate loses a family member, for example, the immediate leader/boss should assume the role of helping that person through that loss, within the context of the work that the person performs. Someone losing his or her job is also a crisis. In these cases, absent evidence of criminal behavior driving the separation, the immediate boss should deliver the bad news. This is not a task for a staff member (like HR), who is outside of the terminated employee's workgroup. Sadly, I have seen some companies' leaders exhibit the evasions of a prison escapee to avoid direct contact with terminated employees. Delivering such news is extremely difficult and unpleasant for most people, but dodging this task is a clear abdication of leadership.[35]

> "We live in a world where facts are less important than narrative, where people emote rather than debate."
> —DAVID PATRIKARAKOS

As difficult as it is to tell someone they are no longer employed, it may be even more challenging to tell someone they are not performing to standard, a task that I have already discussed as one of the most challenging

---

[35] The motion picture, *Up in the Air*, 2009, brilliantly captures the charade of firing people remotely. George Clooney plays a consultant whose specialty is firing people for large corporations.

leadership trials. In our current culture of an exaggerated sense of self and self-worth, today's leaders should expect to encounter great sensitivity when they direct criticism toward any member of a group. As David Patrikarakos' observation (above) suggests, many members of our society seem to have forgotten that employing reason requires hard work and practice; too many people rely on their own emotions as their sole source of judgment. These factors make leading significant improvement efforts increasingly challenging and, sadly, almost as demanding as leading in a crisis. In this situation, the leader must create a shared framework in which standards can first be understood. As I once heard a highly effective leader in the army say to his subordinates: "These are the standards. I am asking for your understanding of them, but not your approval, because these are the standards." I have also observed in countless situations that, as the group performs more successfully, embracing higher standards becomes easier.

The Dunning-Kruger Effect

The importance of leadership and setting standards is underscored by a cognitive bias first defined by social psychologists David Dunning and Justin Kruger in a 1999 study entitled "Unskilled and Unaware of It: How Difficulties in Recognizing One's Own Incompetence Lead to Inflated Self-Assessments."[36] The Dunning-Kruger Effect, so named after the findings of this study, is actually two-fold: incompetent people have a greatly inflated view of their own abilities because they lack an understanding of standards and of where they fall on the spectrum (internal illusion). The other side of the coin is that competent people often overrate the abilities of others because they assume others perform as well as they can (external misperception).

The risk suggested by the Dunning-Kruger Effect is that incompetents don't know what they don't know, and that the competent people erroneously assume greater ability in people less skilled. To avoid creating a tragedy of errors through this effect, leaders in situations

---

[36] The Dunning-Kruger Effect article appeared in *Current Neurology and Neuroscience Reports*. Dec 1999. Accessed February 2019. https://www.ncbi.nim.nih.gov/pubmed/10626367/.

where performance must be improved need to define a clear picture of the standards to be met. This effort must be complemented by defining a clear picture of the current level of performance. Both ends of the performance spectrum, the current standards and the desired standards, must be articulated by the leader and understood by all participants.

Why We Hate Change

Performance improvement is a subset of the larger endeavor of organizational change, a very challenging leadership mission. Having worked in organizational change for most of my adult life, I have distilled a set of observations about why many people in large organizations despise change:

- The lower in the hierarchy you travel in the organization, the more anxiety you sense about change. I believe this is directly related to the lack of control people feel they possess regarding the change process.

- Many so-called change efforts are mere façades for reductions in head count.

- Even if you survive the head count reduction, you'll end up with more work to do, without commensurate compensation.

- Change consultants run around spouting the things you've been saying for years, but no one has listened to you.

This puts great pressure on the leader of any group undergoing significant change. But ironically, change acolytes (and their consultants) high in the organization often damage the prospects of success by heralding *too much* change. Especially for people who don't feel they exercise much control over the change process (which is the vast majority of people in the organization), what they need are dependable anchors from which to base their efforts, not hype about how great the future will be. A capable leader is one of the best anchors.

My own thinking about organizational change has led me to conclude that we make changes to our organizations along a spectrum:

- For quick, one-time changes that affect only one aspect of the endeavor, we *adjust*.

- For more complex changes, to include ongoing incremental changes, we *adapt*.

- For significant changes that are both broad and deep within the organization, we *transform*.

In my life, I have seen few sudden changes that I would deem transformational. The most profound transformational changes have occurred over a span of years. For example, the US Army transformed from a near-dysfunctional organization after the Vietnam War (the early to mid-1970s) into a very effective fighting force over the 1980s, culminating in the magnificent performance in Desert Storm in 1991. In the retail industry, I have observed two models that transformed the industry in the past fifty years: the first was Walmart, whose processes every United States retailer had to imitate to some degree by the 1990s. The second is still happening now, with Amazon and online retailing. These changes are transformational: big muscle movements. But these are few; most change efforts are adjustments or adaptations.

Leaders do a great disservice to their followers when every change is lauded as a life-changing event. Rather, when the word "change" is uttered, followers want to know, in this order:

- How does this affect my job?

- Is this just a flavor-of-the-month, a passing fad?

- Is my leader in this with me?

- What effort will I need to make?

- Will I get the tools and training to make this change successfully?

Sadly, many leaders, especially at higher levels, merely move pieces back and forth to create the illusion of change, conjuring an illusion of progress: centralizing this function or that; organizing by region, then by function, then by product, then beginning the cycle all over again; creating a new staff position. While some of these efforts might be effective, often they simply generate movement without progress. This creates a chasm between the leaders directing the change and the people impacted by it. When people are facing a bad situation and must make difficult changes, the leader needs to imitate the pig in the old saying about ham and eggs: "The chicken was involved, but the pig was committed."

Sharing The Risk And Sharing The Values

When organizations and societies today face daunting challenges, I believe the glue that can hold the group together is sharing risk and sharing values. For example, several factors contribute to a successful army, but capable leadership at the small unit level, where the risk is greatest, is certainly one of them.

I had the privilege of commanding a reinforced tank battalion of more than 700 soldiers in Desert Storm in 1991. After the main fighting, my unit overran an Iraqi Corps headquarters, an entity that controlled thousands of soldiers spread out in units positioned in a wide area. When we overran the headquarters, there was only one Iraqi in the entire area; everyone else had evacuated. The Iraqi, an officer, had been wounded and left behind. As we attended to his wounds (which were not serious), he told us that the headquarters had been bombed during the air war phase, which preceded our ground advance. A few days after the air war had begun, all the officers in this headquarters got into vehicles and rode away, telling the remaining soldiers that they were all going to a meeting. The officers never returned; they had clearly decided to get away but had no compunction about leaving their soldiers behind, in danger. Soon the rest of the soldiers in the headquarters began to melt away, running north into the desert, leaving this wounded officer behind.

I contrast this story with the example of Lee Iacocca at Chrysler Corporation in 1979. At this time, Chrysler was an independent American automobile manufacturer (it was later purchased by Daimler Benz, and then by FIAT). Through a series of spectacular management blunders over the thirty-plus years after World War II, the company was losing prodigious amounts of money. Chrysler was clearly headed for bankruptcy by the late 1970s. Iacocca stepped in as the new CEO and managed to secure loans from the United States government to keep the company afloat. But the loans included serious requirements for the company to restore its health. The granting of these loans was controversial at the time, with some members of Congress from both sides of the aisle decrying the move. While the entire episode was complex and remains controversial (shareholders took a huge haircut, and the workforce was significantly reduced), the company did manage to recover, repaid the loans, and enjoyed profitable years in the 1980s. Most symbolically, Lee Iacocca, the CEO, took only one dollar in salary during the transition. Management followed suit with pay reductions. Everyone knew that if the company emerged successfully from this transition, Lee Iacocca would be handsomely compensated, and he was. However, at the time of the crisis, his example resonated strongly with the employees and with the general public, who were on the hook as taxpayers for the loans.

Concluding With (Who Else) Winston Churchill

Perhaps the most prominent example of leadership in a time of crisis in the past 100 years is Winston Churchill, prime minister of the UK. We must remember the timing of the crisis he and his nation faced: first, Churchill was a washed-up politician in the late 1930s. He joined the cabinet of Prime Minister Neville Chamberlain at the outbreak of World War II in September 1939 as First Lord of the Admiralty, a job from which he had been fired in the First World War. Chamberlain had only called upon Churchill because of the crisis of war, because the leaders of Churchill's own conservative party really didn't trust or like him. When the Germans successfully invaded Norway in 1940, confidence in Chamberlain's leadership dwindled, and Churchill was chosen to lead a national government of all the parties to conduct the war. While Churchill was popular among the British public and the armed forces, many members of his own party remained skeptical. This crisis is brilliantly (and mostly accurately) portrayed in the 2017 movie, *The Darkest Hour*.

Within days of his becoming PM, Churchill and the UK were faced with a grim situation. The German Army attacked the UK's main ally, France, which had been the bulwark against the Germans during World War I. Astoundingly, the Germans quickly overran France. Churchill and the UK were faced with extremely difficult choices: Should they seek some kind of accommodation with Hitler, or should they continue to fight? The Germans had been spectacularly successful in every military campaign to this point. (This all occurred before the German invasion of the Soviet Union in June 1941, where they met their first defeats.) German propaganda had also been very effective in conveying an image of a mighty and efficient German war machine, so many British assumed their own army and air forces were completely outclassed.

While we are still familiar today with Churchill's inspirational speeches to his nation ("blood, toil, tears, and sweat," "never surrender," "their finest hour"), it is often overlooked that Churchill first had to marshal the support of his cabinet, his immediate key group. As I have discussed previously, leaders whose span is huge in scale still must maintain the leadership of their immediate group, that smaller range within Dunbar's Number. Knowing that he had to convince his restless inner circle to support his decision to fight on, Churchill called his outer cabinet, a larger body of twenty-five members, together, and made a brief address that ended with:

"If this long island story of ours is to end at last, let it end only when each one of us lies choking in his own blood upon the ground."

Please note that his graphic words emphasize *us*. The risk belonged to everyone, and Churchill fully accepted that. We know from his memoirs that he was fully prepared to die fighting. His cabinet was inspired by his determination, and they fully backed Churchill's risky decision to fight on. Churchill remarked later on the effect of this small meeting:

"It fell to me in the coming days and months to express their [the cabinet] sentiments [to fight on]...This I was able to do because they were mine also."

The UK managed to fight on as the only major adversary of Nazi Germany for one perilous year thanks to the leadership of Winston Churchill. In 1941, the Soviet Union and the United States became allies of Britain, adding the scale of resources to ultimately defeat Nazi Germany. Obviously, words spoken during a crisis have much more universal appreciation after the fact, when victory has been achieved, than when they are first uttered, as the example of the Gettysburg Address so amply shows. It was equally if not *more* important for Churchill to lead his inner circle in the cause as it was for him to rally the nation with his speeches. Irrespective of his audience, his character exemplified the tenacity to fight on.

Today, eighty years and three generations after Churchill, we can still take inspiration from this example of leadership, which inspired his audiences, first with his colleagues and immediate subordinates, and later with the nation. Churchill didn't shy away from describing the risks and sacrifices ahead. But amid the crisis, he painted a picture of ultimate triumph, and his audience always knew he shared the risk with them. From his first speech as prime minister to the House of Commons, May 13, 1940:

> "We have before us an ordeal of the most grievous kind. We have before us many, many long months of struggle and of suffering. You ask, what is our policy? I will say: It is to wage war, by sea, land and air, with all our might and with all the strength that God can give us; to wage war against a monstrous tyranny, never surpassed in the dark and lamentable catalogue of human crime. That is our policy. You ask, what is our aim? I can answer in one word: victory; victory at all costs, victory in spite of all terror, victory, however long and hard the road may be; for without victory, there is no survival...But I take up my task with buoyancy and hope. I feel sure that our cause will not be suffered to fail among men. At this time I feel

entitled to claim the aid of all, and I say, 'Come then, let us go forward together with our united strength.'"

In 1940, the people of Britain turned to Churchill as their leader in a crisis, and he met the challenge. We recall today the stirring speeches, disseminated by broadcast and print technology, but we should also remember the importance of Churchill leading his political base, the core of his political party. Still, the example of Churchill just three years later also shows how the situation can change and alter a leader's effectiveness.

When Leadership Roles Change

Sir Edgar Williams told me about a November 1943 meeting he observed between Churchill and the US Army Chief of Staff, General George C. Marshall, in Cairo, Egypt. At this point, the United States was assuming the role of senior partner in the war, since the United States was now employing more men, money, and equipment to fight. The purpose of the meeting was to decide the grand strategy for engaging and defeating Germany in the near future, with the invasion of France looming. Sir Edgar related that Churchill went into full Churchillian speaking mode (striding, holding his lapels, and gesticulating grandly) in describing how the Allies must invade the island of Rhodes in the Mediterranean, a location rather removed from main effort. At this point General Marshall (a man who Sir Edgar said possessed incredible moral power and who rarely cursed) said bluntly that no American was going to die on "that goddamned island." Sir Edgar said Churchill responded like a balloon that had been deflated. He simply sat down and meekly acquiesced.

Historians have called George Marshall the only general Churchill ever feared. Marshall was not going to let anything dilute the effort for the upcoming invasion of Normandy, and he had the power (through his presence and his authority as chief of staff of the US Army, and having the full confidence of President Roosevelt) not to be swayed by Churchill's oratory and stubbornness. Churchill was truly the man of the hour in 1940 and 1941. By late 1943, however, the situation had changed. He was no longer the principal leader in the fight against Nazi

Germany, no longer the focus of the great effort. He was now the junior partner in a coalition. The context had changed dramatically, and so had his leadership role.

Churchill was the master of the spoken and written word, and he was one of the rare cases where a leader at a very high level of the organization—an executive—frequently exercised direct contact with the mass of his followers. Technology today has made it even easier to communicate directly to the masses, but does this really put the high-level leader closer to his or her followers?

CHAPTER 11

The Digital Delusion

THE PREVAILING POPULAR VIEW: *"Today we live in a time of unprecedented change." "Digitization has revolutionized our relationships."*

TOUGH LOVE REALITY: *More profound changes to society occurred one hundred and fifty years ago. Digitization has not changed our fundamental relationships today.*

Winston Churchill was a magnificent communicator in his speeches, but his oratorical skill was closely linked to his writing prowess, since he read from his notes during his speeches. The power of his voice and his words were magnified by the technology of the day, radio, whose use as a mass medium was less than twenty years old in the dark days of 1940 (the BBC was founded in 1927). Today, leaders are confronted with new technology, or rather, a series of related technologies driven by digitization: the conversion of data into tiny, discrete units, or bits, so that information can be transmitted and then reconstructed on a staggeringly large scale. In older, analog technology, information was transmitted in a form that mirrored its original state, but digital devices tear the information down and then remake it. This ability to reduce and then recreate information gives this technology enormous scale: the amount of information processed, the breadth of its dissemination, and the speed of this process far exceed the capabilities of analog technology.

Myths Of Change

When discussing new technologies today, we often say we're in an age of great and constant change, but I would caution us all against believing we are special today with respect to change. As humans, we tend to overestimate the significance of the present because we have a bias toward the immediate moment.[37] Our focus on the current moment is reflected in our widespread belief that no previous era was as innovative and dynamic as our world today.

My contrarian view about change is this: Our lives today are not as buffeted by changes in technology as we think they are, especially when compared to earlier generations. A simple exercise in human memory should persuade us. Compare your lifespan with those of your parents, grandparents, and great-grandparents. For example, here is my lifespan compared to the male line, extending back three generations:

- Timothy T. Lupfer   1950—present (and *much* further, I hope)

- David A. Lupfer (father)   1922-2017

- Loren L. Lupfer (grandfather)   1892-1984

- Arthur H. Lupfer (great-grandfather)   1857-1957

When I consider the changes that occurred within the lifetimes of my great-grandfather or my grandfather, I can make no claim on having been impacted by the *greatest* technological changes. Whether in the areas of technology, health, or communications, my life has neither been as greatly disrupted nor as greatly enhanced during my lifetime as the lives of my great-grandfather, grandfather, or even my father. In almost every area, my life has been more predictable and consistent than the lives of those who went before me. My great-grandfather saw food production (farming and distribution) go from how it had been done for thousands of years (using human and animal power, and hideously inefficient distribution systems) to mechanization, refrigeration, and global distribution. My

---

[37] Yagoda, Ben. "Your Lying Mind: The Cognitive Biases Tricking Your Brain." *The Atlantic*. Atlantic Media Company, August 7, 2018. https://www.theatlantic.com/magazine/archive/2018/09/cognitive-bias/565775/.

grandfather saw humans take flight, from the Wright Brothers to landing on the moon. My life experiences can't match those.

The Big Jump In Our Lifetime—Digitization

This begs the question: what has been the most profound technological change in my lifetime? When I consider what changes have occurred in technology since 1950, the change that emerges most strongly is digitization, and that is the subject of this chapter, especially if this innovation will change the nature of leadership. But I suggest that the impact of digitization has not yet been fully felt; we have years, perhaps generations, to go before the full impact of digitization is realized.

What has digitization achieved thus far?

- We can collect, store, analyze, and disseminate information on a scale impossible before digitization.

- The availability of information is profoundly greater than in the past.

- The scale of transmission of information is almost unlimited.

- The scale of analysis of available information is almost unlimited.

- The costs of digital communications are much lower than analog communications.

Digital technology has spawned numerous innovations, from hardware (smartphones, personal computers, tablets, servers) to software (from utility applications to video games) to global social communications channels (Twitter, Instagram, Facebook, LinkedIn, etc.) to completely new forms of retailing and commerce (most notably Amazon and Alibaba). We have all become increasingly reliant on this technology. On most surveys, responses are significantly more favorable than unfavorable regarding the use of digital communications.[38] However, calls for reconsidering our dependence on digital technology (some even call it an *addiction*) are increasing in number and intensity.[39]

---

[38] "Digital Media and Society: Implications in a Hyperconnected Era." *World Economic Forum*. Accessed February 13, 2019. https://www.weforum.org/reports/digital-media-and-society-implications-in-a-hyperconnected-era.

[39] An example of such an analysis is Turkle, Sherry. *Alone Together: Why We Expect More From Technology and Less from Each Other*. New York: Basic Books, a member of the Perseus Books Group, 2012.

The Digital Downsides

At the micro level, critics note how distracted digital users can be, and especially how digital users could become removed from basic, direct interaction with people, to the detriment of establishing and maintaining healthy relationships. Like complaints sixty years ago about adolescents watching television, critics today maintain that children and adolescents are spending excessive and damaging amounts of time with digital devices, from video games to smartphones. These complaints cite problems for chronic digital users in adjusting to the real, nondigital environment by pointing to deficiencies in direct communication and maintaining relationships.

These specific problems would likely exist irrespective of user motivations, but the next set of digitization criticisms arise from users whose motives are questionable. These problems include a false sense of empowerment and importance, in that digitization gives unfiltered access to various digital media and can connect individuals to a much greater audience than in analog days. People with malicious intent can broadcast while remaining distant and untraceable, protected from the people they attack. Whether a participant in digital communications is malevolent or ill-informed, or both, he or she can express him- or herself without the institutional constraints (editors, boards, reviewers, sponsors, organizational restrictions) that have previously existed for other forms of mass communication.

The macro level of communications perhaps raises the most disturbing concerns. For a variety of reasons, the printed word formerly enjoyed a patina of immediate credibility, because we assumed some amount of scrutiny had occurred before the expense of printing and distributing the message had been incurred. Today, expressing yourself in "print" on the internet is costless, largely uncensored, and generally unedited, so vast amounts of inaccurate, deceptive, and utterly nasty material is available to almost anyone to disseminate in the West.

Ironically for an invention that emerged from the US Defense Advanced Research Projects Agency (DARPA) in the early 1970s, the internet is today being weaponized effectively by countries outside the

West. China is mastering the ability of its central government to control and, when needed, suppress individual expressions on the internet that run counter to the party line. Russia has revitalized the Soviet concept of disinformation and turned it into a digital art form, most evident in its attempts to intimidate Ukraine and the Baltic states by disseminating deceptive digital information and disrupting their systems, and also by sowing mischief in the United States during the 2016 election (the extent of which has yet to be determined).

Leaders And Digitization

So, into this cauldron of the most important technological advances in the last fifty years, with its contrasting potential for both good and ill, jump today's leaders. How does digitization affect leadership today and into the immediate future? Does digitization allow a leader to touch more people personally and directly? Does digitization reduce the need for levels in the hierarchy because of the much greater scale of communications?

First, I must address some basic issues surrounding leaders employing new technology. Irrespective of age or technological background, leaders must *always* keep up with the latest technology that impacts society at large. George H. W. Bush, the forty-first president of the United States, was pilloried by the press and the opposing party when he saw a grocery store scanner during the 1992 presidential election and was "amazed." A review of the videotape (available online) and the background of his visit to the grocers' convention (*not* a supermarket) reveals that Bush was actually not ignorant of the existence of supermarket scanners, but no matter, because the damage from the story was effective: Bush lost the election, and the video of his supposed ignorance of technology certainly didn't help.

In the technology adoption life cycle, leaders should be early adopters or, at a minimum, in the early majority of users of new technology that affects the enterprise—especially new communication technology.[40] Direct digital communication from leaders ensures an unchanged, unedited, unembellished message reaches a broad audience.

---

[40] The technology adoption life cycle was first articulated in the 1950s, and it describes how different groups react to new technology: innovators, early adapters, early majority, late majority, and laggards.

There is no "playing telephone" with the potential for distortion at each communication transfer point. Digitization's scale and directness give the communicator the advantage of consistency and message control (even though it may not do much for the quality of the message).

But the most urgent question is, how does digital communication influence leadership? Does the ability to communicate directly to a large number of followers broaden the number of close relationships the leader can maintain? Does digitization bust Dunbar's Number? My answer is no. Despite our two most recent presidents using Twitter accounts, I do not see a technological change enabling a leader to extend the radius of subordinates with whom he or she can have a close personal relationship. Digitization can certainly expand the range of *distant* followers with whom the leader can "converse" digitally, but the limitations of our brains will continue to constrain the number of true relationships we can maintain.

More Is Not Always Better

Let us consider the limitations of the recipients of digital messages: followers. While Facebook limits the number of Facebook friends to 5,000, reality (Dunbar's Number) limits you to far fewer true friends. Most studies today indicate that however many Facebook friends you rack up, the number of relationships with a genuine connection (where people express concern, where people offer help, etc.) remains limited. This limitation is in line with the general limitations of our brains regarding such key operations as sensory input and processing information.[41] When a leader communicates to a subordinate, the subordinate is going to attach greater importance to that communication than to most others. But a constant barrage of messages, even from the boss, could become annoying and distracting. Constant communication from a leader also can erode the sense of autonomy that most people in free societies desire in their own work, as well as the autonomy of intermediate leaders

---

[41] Perhaps the most famous examination of the limits of our capacity to process information was by psychologist George A. Miller of Harvard in his seminal article, "The Magical Number Seven, Plus or Minus Two: Some Limits on our Capacity for Processing Information," *Psychological Review*, 1956. Although the numbers to describe our limitations are constantly debated, the major point that our brains are limited in their capacity is generally accepted.

between followers and the top leader. Messages, however well intended, can also seem intrusive. I had a recent conversation with someone who had suffered the loss of a sibling. She received a letter of condolence from her state senator, which was certainly appreciated. However, the letter implied a close relationship between the state senator and the recipient that was not accurate; the recipient had only met the state senator once, and very briefly. The state senator had clearly had his staff do a bit of homework to get all the facts correct (using quick access to digitized information), but it was presented in a way that made my friend feel "creepy." However much the recipient appreciated the sentiment behind the letter, at the same time, she found the message disconcerting and intrusive.

Communications always carry a degree of risk to the relationship. In addition to being potentially intrusive, communications between leaders and followers can also become too familiar. An effective leader, in exercising authority, maintains a delicate balance between shared experiences and values (the key personal link between the leader and followers), and a reasonable distance from followers (since unpleasant decisions will always occur). This balance between familiarity and distance will vary based on culture, but it will always be present in some manner in leader/follower relationships.

When I taught history at West Point, Lieutenant General Andrew Goodpaster, the superintendent, described the desired balance in the relationship between officers and cadets as "dignified friendliness," a representation I found helpful as an instructor.

Another description of a much greater gap between leaders and followers was Walter Bagehot's caution in Victorian Britain not to make the British monarchy too familiar, too personalized. In his book, *The English Constitution* (1873), he said of the monarchy: "Its mystery is its life. We must not let in daylight upon magic."[42] In any organizational relationship between leaders and followers, which ultimately should be based on defined differences in decision-making authority, the leader

---

[42] Bagehot, Walter. *The English Constitution*, 1873 (republished in 2007 by Cosimo, Inc., New York, NY).

does not want to dilute the potency of his or her authority. Too much communication can trivialize the leader, sloppy communication can erode respect, and petty communication can delegitimize the leader's position. Leaders should communicate messages appropriate for their level, from subject matter to style.

Leaders at high levels can also undercut their own subordinate leaders by constantly doing an "end around" junior leaders through broad digital communication. While we possess the technology to communicate more directly, we still do not possess the technology to automate, centralize, and solve every problem, as anyone who has tried to get *human* help to solve a complicated problem discovers on an automated helpline. We still need leaders on the ground, and they are not well served by *their* leaders pretending to be the source of all wisdom and truth through digitization. Digitization can certainly reduce the number of levels in an organization through automation, but it will never eliminate them. Basic leadership principles, exercised by contact between leaders and followers, still apply. We still need that immediate leader whom we know, working in the realm of pure leadership; that key zone where leaders and followers have genuine relationships.

The Double-Edged Binary Sword

In addition to being useful tools for expanding leader communications, digital capabilities also present significant new risks. Just as digitization enables a leader to broadcast a clear, consistent message, it also enables a malicious agent to broadcast disinformation, even in the guise of a legitimate leader. From outright fabrications to behavior taken completely out of context and broadcast widely, digital risks could consume today's leaders full time as they constantly address false accusations and misperceptions.

At the same time, the intense scrutiny of our digitized age can also reveal real flaws in any leader, news of which can now be disseminated with incredible speed. As the first presidential debates in American history showed in 1960, the visual broadcast image could either be a tremendous asset (Kennedy) or a significant disadvantage (Nixon). Now that images can be distributed with even greater speed and efficiency, control of a leader's image has become both more important and more challenging. In the past few years, several politicians and executives have been brought down following revelations about ethnic slurs, disdain for perceived "lower" classes, or most recently, sexist behavior toward women. In many of these cases, digital technology was the accelerant in their downfall. Any image or written message that can be captured digitally is now fair game; for prominent leaders, there is no privacy. To add to the digital risks for leaders, photos and videos can now be *distorted* with incredible skill; I predict we will see concocted, false images, which will appear compelling (and seemingly real) more frequently.[43] Today we are just experiencing the beginning of the problems with digitization and its impact on individuals. The potential problems on an organizational scale are daunting as well.

Digital Temptations And Risks

Organizational leaders can fall into the trap of thinking that digitization is the ideal tool for expanding spans of control, which in turn leads to that favorite blunt instrument for reducing costs: cutting personnel. But we shouldn't spread people out so much in our organizations that real relationships cannot be formed. We must remember that we're wired to be visual. We cannot enlarge the span of control so widely that real leadership relationships cannot be established within it. Digitization, like any other technology, is best used as a complement to effective leadership, not a substitute for it.

Another, more serious threat to leadership abides in digitization: As artificial intelligence (AI) progresses, more endeavors, from taking orders to diagnosing complex problems, will automate data analysis and decision-making, thereby reducing the number of humans involved, which will subsequently reduce opportunities to lead. I predict that the ratio of specialists to leaders in organizations will grow larger as a result.

---

[43] For an example how Artificial Intelligence is already capable of creating fake news, please see how comedian Jordan Peele uses AI to make a fake presentation by Barack Obama at:
https://www.theverge.com/tldr/2018/4/17/17247334/ai-fake-news-video-barack-obama-jordan-peele-buzzfeed

This trend will make the future selection and development of leaders more challenging; first, because opportunities to lead will become more scarce, and second, because specialists, especially highly paid specialists, can be notably difficult to lead.

No magic technological invention will make anyone a better leader. Instead, leaders are developed through the process articulated by the New York taxi driver who, when asked by a frantic passenger, "How do I get to Carnegie Hall," responded, "Practice, practice, practice."

What Is To Be Done?
Applying Leadership Tough Love
To Individuals

**Advice From The Virtuous
Machiavelli To The Individual
Aspiring To Be A Leader—
How To Ensure That
Character Will Count**

n these final two chapters, I wish to offer advice to both individuals and organizations about leadership. In doing so, I shall assume the persona of the Virtuous Machiavelli: describing the world as it really is, while encouraging the practice of virtue in encountering that world.

The encouragement of virtue has a long pedigree in Western culture, with deep roots both in the ancient writings of Greece and Rome and from Judaism and Christianity. Also, that perceived scourge of virtue, Machiavelli, may perhaps not have been as "Machiavellian" as we commonly assume. From the span of time across five centuries, we simply don't know Machiavelli's intent in writing his most famous work, *The Prince.* While he appears utterly cynical in that work, he celebrated virtue in many of his other works (such as *The Art of War*), so we are uncertain about the divergence in his writings regarding virtue. Perhaps he wrote *The Prince* to provide a stark warning of what power looks like without the restraint of virtue. Although the word *virtue* today sounds outmoded, I attempt to revive it through the element of character. This revival is not some yearning for a mythical past, but a practical search for better leadership on two levels:

- Virtue, or character, has inherent value to the leader and to followers; it is good in itself. All societies recognize some basic behaviors as fundamentally good and desirable.[44]

- In any collection of people, decision-making authority will always vary, and material differences (possessions) will always create inequalities in status as well. But shared goals and values are the binding forces for group cohesion—forces that can overcome differences in status. Character (or virtue) is the egalitarian thread that should run through all groups, with shared values linking inspiring leadership with the discretionary effort of followers, and ultimately with cumulative improvement—a decidedly *practical* reason for fostering character in leaders.

Not Everyone Is A Leader In An Organization

These final two chapters begin with a reiteration of one of my basic leadership insights: not everyone is a leader, not everyone wants to be a leader, and not everyone should be a leader. Many talented, exceptional people want to concentrate on their chosen specialties and do not want to take on the heavy responsibilities of leading people. Wise organizations will acknowledge and act upon this insight by not forcing leadership roles, especially at the higher levels, upon those who lack the desire, ability, or experience to lead. We also have all met people who have the ambition to lead, but who lack the basic savvy to direct other people, who grossly overestimate their own abilities, or whose complete self-absorption leaves no values with which to connect to anyone else.

Situations certainly exist in which the role of leader is forced upon people, whether they seek the role or not. The most frequent instance is in the family. In the nuclear family, parents become leaders, simply because young humans require leadership during their long progress to

---

[44] I used the research of Jonathan Haidt earlier in chapter 4 to suggest six fundamental values for leaders, based on his moral foundations theories.

adulthood. Unfortunately, some parents evade family leadership roles by avoiding them altogether, either waiting for institutions to pick up the role or by ignoring their leadership roles and treating their children simply as small adults or peers (which they definitely are not, neither physically nor neurologically). While a discussion of family leadership is beyond the scope of this book (indeed, it should be the subject of an entire book in itself), I earnestly hope that this general discussion of leadership will influence parents in their thinking about perhaps the most important leadership role of all.

Let us turn now to the case of an individual in an organization who encounters her or his first opportunity to lead.

Leadership Advice From The Virtuous Machiavelli: To The Individual

How should an individual who aspires to be a leader accept the challenge and succeed while working in an organization? First, take on the responsibility for your own leadership development, because most organizations do not engage in this vital activity competently. In most cases, leadership development programs either don't exist (leaders are taught to swim by throwing them in the deep end), or the organization trots out an ever-changing list of "magic" traits, following the latest fads. Rather, *you* must examine yourself, the organizational context, and the goals to be achieved and then apply the three key elements of leadership to your situation.

Let us employ the revised leadership model to guide the process:

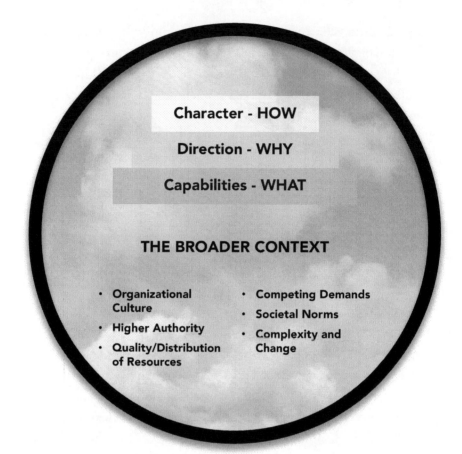

First, examine the broader context. Examining yourself, the challenge, and the organizational culture, consider:

- Are you already using the world as your laboratory, observing how people lead and how followers respond?

- Do you have a genuine desire to lead, not just a desire to enjoy status and power?

- Can you play a cultural anthropologist? Especially if you are new to the organization, you must quickly gauge the values within the culture.

- If the background of the group you lead is mixed, or if the entire culture is foreign to you, how are you going to find common ground?

- How does the mission of your group fit into the larger context? How vital is this effort compared to other demands on the larger organization?

- How turbulent is the organization? If the situation is extremely fluid, how can you frame the situation to create some psychological stability for you and your followers?

- Assess your new leadership role: What authority do you possess? While authority is not a club with which to beat people down, it *is* a vital tool that you must be prepared to use. You must know its dimensions for your role.

Next, evaluate your boss:

- Do you have any influence on the choice of the person for whom you will work? If so, always try to work for someone with a solid reputation as a leader. Working for a toxic leader should be avoided wherever possible, irrespective of that person's power and influence.

- Do you have the strength of will to turn down the golden opportunity to work with a tyrant? Always be wary of a leader who denies the importance or existence of his or her followers' own self-interest. This leader's interests will become the *only* interests of the effort.

Consider the people you will lead and the resources you will manage:

- What talent are you working with? Can you obtain an unvarnished assessment of the caliber of talent in the group you are leading?

- Who are your direct reports? What combination of authority and influence can you employ most successfully? If the followers' relationships with your leadership role do not involve formal, direct reporting, what kind of relationships do you have, and what authority can you leverage?

- What tensions have emerged in the group before your arrival?

- What influence skills are necessary for your role? What influence skills need to be developed or honed?

- Can you get into the sympathetic listening mode? Solicit followers' assessments and comments as early as possible—and filter them.

- Do you have sufficient resources to accomplish the mission? If you feel there is a deficit, raise this issue immediately with your boss.

Assess the key element of direction:

- What is the purpose of your group's effort? How do you define success, and how does the organization and your immediate boss define success? How would your team define success?

- Can you articulate the endeavor's direction to achieve the best balance:

   - to line up your followers' self-interest with the organizational goals?

   - to place everyone's efforts in the context of the greater purpose?

- Can you achieve a general understanding of the measures of success?

> A story is told about President Kennedy visiting NASA in 1962: He asked a janitor what he was doing, and the janitor responded, "Well, Mr. President, I'm helping put a man on the moon." Someone at NASA certainly knew how to link everyone's efforts to the big picture.

Evaluate the key element of capabilities:

- Can you gauge your own abilities as dispassionately as possible? Carefully assess the capabilities demanded in your leadership role. To address any serious gaps, find solutions immediately—source talent within the group, bring in temporary expertise, extract wisdom from an industry veteran or coach, etc.

- Can you balance between being observant and being hands-on? If you are new to the group and the organization, be more hands-on at first and then allow more autonomy as your confidence in the group's abilities increases.

- Regarding the larger context of your group's effort: Can you communicate more about the context, not less? Always share the bigger picture by letting different groups or individuals know what other groups and individuals are doing. Cross-knowledge is an excellent development tool for all members of the group, especially for future leaders.

- Can you distinguish between form and substance? Do not confuse capabilities with style. Every human has his or her own personality, and all people need to find the style of interaction most effective for them, as long as it stays within the bounds of behavioral norms and shared values.

- Do you have the confidence to give subordinate leaders autonomy in their roles as leaders? Do not suck the leadership oxygen out of the air, depriving everyone else of a meaningful leadership role.

- Can you identify problems and intervene effectively? Be precise and quick on performance corrections. In counseling for improvement, focus on the observed actions, not on the personality or presumed intent.

- Have you got the stomach to deliver bad news, in any direction within the hierarchy: down, across, and up? Never side-step that duty when it is required.

> Deng Xiaoping brought more people out of poverty than any other person in the twentieth century by removing the shackles of Maoist ideology and unleashing the pursuit of happiness for over one billion people. One of his favorite sayings was that it doesn't make any difference if the cat is black or white, as long as it catches mice.

Finally, examine the key element of character:

- Are you genuine in your expressions of values? Link values to actions when appropriate; do not force it, however, for the effort will appear clumsy.

- Are you aware of the magnification on you in your role? Remember that you, as a leader, will be constantly scrutinized for maintaining values—do not disappoint. Remember my proposed basic values of fairness, lack of malice, loyalty to the group and its mission, deference to authority and standards, aspiration to be unsullied, and encouragement of autonomy.

- Can you handle the inevitable ambiguity of moral issues? Learn to address ethical dilemmas and explain decisions made in those circumstances. Be ready to admit when you face a difficult ethical trade-off.

- Will you quickly call out behaviors that undermine values? Be alert for rumblings about hypocrisy, especially when they may apply to you.

- Can you assess character in others quickly and effectively? Focus on behaviors, not talk. Never confuse character with likeability.[45] Assessing character has a high Carnegie Hall Factor—it requires plenty of practice, practice, practice.

---

[45] Likeability is recognized as the common heuristic for selections, whether in a job interview or in voting. It must be true, for I have seen so many unlikeable politicians strive mightily to appear likeable.

- Have you developed the maturity to recognize that tensions and disagreements are not automatically issues of character? Intelligent, well-intentioned people can and will disagree. Learn to distinguish between a disagreement about the method and when a value is at risk.

The Challenge

For an example of how these insights could apply to a leadership opportunity in a larger organization, let us use a mundane but common situation: You have recently joined the organization and are asked to lead a committee. This is your first shot at a leadership role in this organization, and although the task seems minor, you want to do the best you can. Leading requires a healthy ego and a non-fragile personality to work through inevitable tension. Let us assume that you believe that you're up for the challenge.

Setting Yourself Up For Success

The detailed context: You have recently joined a midsized organization of 300 people. Your role is as an individual contributor, such as an analyst, but as you perform well in that role (because you must first deliver in that role and demonstrate individual competence), you remain alert for opportunities to lead. Be aware, however, of the difference between exerting influence and leading. You may have been directed to "work with this client and get them to…" or "find out from this regulator what X really means…" Your boss may even have called these efforts *leading*, but they were not, unless you had subordinates to help you. If you, alone, were tasked with influencing someone, recognize that these efforts, however important they may have been, were not leadership.

But now you have received the call: "We are forming this committee to accomplish X, and we want you to lead it." Now there is a goal with your name on it, and some people whom you must lead to accomplish it. The first step is to understand the goal and what constitutes success. You certainly should determine what *you* believe success is, but you should also have a clear picture of success in the eyes of whoever gave you the mission. Quickly assess how challenging the task is: Have several people already tried and failed, or is this a reachable goal?

The more delicate question is what authority you possess to accomplish the goal. Not wanting to appear power-hungry, you are not going to ask directly, but you can subtly gauge what tools you have. First, do any members of the committee work directly for you? Let us assume not: Welcome to the challenge of responsibility without much authority, a common scenario at lower levels of organizations. Never deceive yourself into thinking that your amazing personality alone will get you through, or that the importance of the mission will inspire everyone to cooperate. Tensions will exist, and dysfunction is always a risk.

Because you want to succeed, you will utilize all the tools you can, and that includes extracting whatever form of authority you can muster. Assume that you shall have to overcome some tension in leading the effort. Any form of authority, deftly employed, will complement your influencing skills and improve the odds of success.

Generate some *reflected authority* by invoking the higher-level boss who formed the committee in the first place. Have that person open the first meeting, whether digitally or in person, with a statement regarding why this effort is being made, and that you are responsible for leading it. Offline, obtain private assurances that you can turn to the big boss for advice when you need it—a useful arrow to keep in your quiver. Most likely you possess the authority to put the agenda together. Most busy people (and we all claim to be very busy) are only too happy to have someone else create an agenda when they are not in charge. Assess your committee and develop approaches to generate momentum in the right direction, such as putting the most easily resolved issues first.

Let us assume this effort is not fluff; rather, this group has been assembled for a genuine purpose, to address a real issue. Be zealous in leading the group and focusing on the goal, but agnostic about the specific path to get there. Empirical evidence strongly points to the benefit of diverse opinions in problem-solving; groupthink reduces both friction *and* effective solutions, so try to avoid conditions that encourage it, even though reaching consensus quickly may appear easier. Instead, calmly and deliberately take in all reasonable ideas. Open all meetings, irrespective of the media, with confidence, stating their clear purpose and the process for achieving meeting goals. Always be organized, and when you (rarely) aren't, always *appear* organized. Get buy-in for ground rules and try to place restrictions on the use of digital devices and other distractors and interruptions, so they do not disrupt your proceedings. Even if you have a wild and crazy group that makes you feel you are herding cats, as the leader, you should manage the time to keep the effort on time and on point.

If it is all running fairly smoothly, keep a steady focus on the goal, and keep scope creep and other wanderings under control. Keep everyone—followers and bosses—aware of the progress. When the work is finished, and your group effort is successful, celebrate the success with some sort of group recognition and invite the boss who assigned you the mission. Remember who was effective in your group and stay in touch with them. Then be ready to move on to the next leadership opportunity.

But what if someone in your group was a proverbial pain in the gluteus maximus?

Managing Bad Behavior

In our scenario, where you're leading a committee with little formal authority, you may encounter a participant who is difficult. Since you lack formal authority to remove him or her from the group yourself, you must try other approaches.

Once evidence is clear that this person is not cooperating (he or she may be absent, inattentive, annoyed at the duty, envious that you're in charge, or all of the above), you cannot wish the problem away. If this person is going to put your success at risk, act on it quickly. First, communicate directly with that person (face-to-face is best). Clearly state that this person does not seem to be well-engaged, and ask if anything you are doing is creating the problem. This question is not a throwaway line; you actually may be doing something to create the problem, despite your best intentions. More importantly, by opening the discussion this way, you are not putting this person completely on the defensive as you address this problem. You're *sharing* the problem (even though deep down you may think this person is a jerk).

Let's assume the person utters a few vague phrases, and you both come to an agreement to work better together, but later behavior demonstrates this person hasn't changed, and things are now getting to be dysfunctional within the committee. Now you must act decisively. You've given a good faith effort, and it has failed. You will either endure the problem, or you will try to get this person off the committee.

You opt for the latter choice because the success of the effort demands a change. You carefully gather all the facts and go to the authority who can change out the members of your group. Your approach should be unambiguous: It is in the best interest of accomplishing the task you have given us that so-and-so be replaced. Let the higher authority then ask questions of you, and provide the facts in an unemotional manner. You may be asked if other members feel the same way about this person. Circumstances will vary in each case, but in general, I recommend that this *not* be a subject for group discussion or individual interviews. You are tasked with leading, and this is an issue that affects *you* and the success of the entire effort. The higher authority may advise giving the problem some time (a common delaying tactic before making a decision), but then you should set a time limit with him or her, beyond which action must be taken.

The higher authority could also say that he or she will talk with this person to get her or him to cooperate better. Any number of outcomes are now possible, from excellent (the higher authority puts the fear of God in the difficult person) to disastrous (unbeknownst to you, the higher authority is very close to this person).

If the higher authority agrees that the person will be replaced, you can now soften the blow (and help the higher authority) by having a suggested reason ready: This person's job requires such demanding work, he or she simply can't devote more time to this project, and another person from that division will now join the effort. It will all sound nice;

no one is humiliated, but other members of the committee will catch on and will most likely behave better too.

One disruptive person can cause immense damage to any group, making leadership unpleasant and potentially unproductive. When your name is on the result, and your authority is weak, to solve such a serious problem you must leverage the authority of others to remove the source of the problem. This is always a risky course of action. Also, this approach is like the sting of a bee—you can only do this *once* while leading an effort where your authority is limited.

Who Is My Entourage?

Besides ambiguity of authority, another factor that makes leading at lower organizational levels more difficult than at higher levels is that the selection of subordinates is more restricted at lower levels. Since leadership opportunities should begin as early as possible in a career, new leaders will most likely have followers assigned, not selected. This provides the new leader with important lessons in how to judge followers' capabilities and character. New leaders should learn quickly how to spot the different levels of adherence in their subordinates: fully on board, skeptical but complying, openly resisting, and the most difficult of all—fake compliance with behind-the-scenes resistance. Just as followers within the circle of close relationships will assess the leader's competence, so will the leader assess each subordinate. To determine who can be trusted, the new leader will compare what each follower says with what each one does, and the followers will do the same with the leader.

After an experience with an incompetent or untrustworthy follower, a leader will always try to select her or his immediate subordinates whenever possible. This is a natural desire, for already having a relationship with someone and knowing the pros and cons reduces considerable work at the outset of a project or new position. This practice can result, however, in a leader at higher levels moving into new positions with a small army of loyal supporters—a practice I firmly believe should be limited.

What Constitutes Good Leadership Experiences For You?

What leadership assignments are the most rewarding? That depends on the nature of the effort. Leading in a crisis is the most demanding role, but for most of us, crises will arise unpredictably, whether a family crisis (unexpected death in the family) or an external bolt (economic crisis). In the professions where crises occur frequently—both within our own society (emergency rooms, police, firefighters, first responders, etc.) or outside our borders (the military)—the ability to remain calm and to direct action is paramount. For those of us who do not face these challenges frequently, running our own mental simulations of how we would respond in a crisis is a useful exercise, for we do not want to be found wanting when a crisis occurs on our watch.

But for all leaders in today's society, shaping up a group's performance will remain the most frequent significant leadership challenge. As I recalled with my friend who was hired to improve the performance of a group of highly trained specialists and who was then thrown under the bus for doing his job, the leader accepting this challenge must ensure first that higher leadership is fully supportive, to include being able to withstand initial, inevitable complaints and threats from disgruntled followers. Inspiring leadership can create wonderful cooperation between the leader and the led, but it often requires a bumpy ride to get there. Just as many iconic television shows (*Seinfeld*, for example) required months, sometimes an entire season, to develop a loyal following, so do leaders (particularly those leading a new group or a group in the need of serious revision in either performance or behavior) require time to establish themselves and standards going forward.

What About My Boss?

To succeed in almost any organization, you must please your immediate boss, and if that is impossible, you had better be *very* friendly with the boss the next level up. Regrettably, in too many hierarchies, pleasing the boss propels promotions more than effective leadership, although in the best of circumstances, the two are not mutually exclusive. Just as the likeability of the candidate influences hiring decisions more than any other factor, so does pleasing the boss help people ascend the organizational ladder. Should the aspiring leader strive to please his or her immediate superior? Absolutely. Just remember that this is not leadership. Most importantly, when *you* evaluate your subordinates who are leaders, never forget that this skill, often called *managing upward*, is not leadership.

The importance of influence also applies to peers and other collaborators (regulators, customers, suppliers, etc.). It is simply common sense to maintain good relationships wherever possible, because relationships in our society are (or should be) reciprocal, and no one can predict when these relationships may be needed to help with a given problem.

My final advice on your immediate boss is for all leaders to perform the Best Leader Exercise constantly. Find out who is considered an outstanding leader in the organization and learn from him or her, even if you can't work for that person directly. Effective leaders attract good, talented followers; this characteristic separates them from the tyrant or bully who ekes out short-term or fake success by chewing people up and spitting them out. If you have an immediate boss who is an outstanding leader, savor the experience, because leadership is best learned by apprenticing to an outstanding leader.

But what if your boss is not a paragon of excellent leadership?

The one situation in which the influential relationship with your boss can be utterly debilitating is when the immediate boss is an obviously ineffective leader because of incompetence, misbehavior, or immorality (or all of the above). Please note that I did not say criminal; when you believe that is the situation, the actions required are well defined: Make a record of your observations and get out from under that boss as fast as you can. In the case of the noncriminal IMI boss (*i*ncompetent, *m*isbehaving, and/or *i*mmoral), you can try to ride it out, escape to another position, or find relief by appealing to higher authority. If you are fortunate enough to have a sterling reputation, you can threaten to resign unless this boss is removed; be prepared, however, to follow through and resign if your bluff is called. If you do not possess such a strong reputation, you run a serious risk when you appeal to the next higher level—greater than the risk of appealing to the authority to remove someone from your team, described earlier. When you go around your immediate boss's back, you are being disloyal. I would argue that an IMI boss is not worthy of such loyalty, but arguments about the obligations of loyalty to higher authority have been raging since rebellions against monarchs in the West in the seventeenth century, to include a certain rebellion in 1776. As our founding fathers knew, rebelling against established authority is incredibly dangerous, and while we won't be drawn and quartered today for such a rebellion, we can certainly lose our jobs. I have seen more good leaders derailed in their careers by a bad boss than any other factor. Whenever you can, choose your boss carefully.

What About Failure?

One of the harshest lessons for decent people trying to lead is that good intentions alone do not guarantee success. An achievable purpose (direction) and the ability to employ resources (capabilities) are essential elements for any leader to succeed. Character is the secret sauce to inspire extra effort and to sustain long-term success. But to be effective, character rests on direction and capabilities. And even with those three key elements solidly in place, things can still go wrong. External factors, like a hailstorm before the harvest, can ruin everything. Unexpected internal changes, such as the loss of a key group member, can throw the best plans in turmoil. In these situations, the depth of the leader's resilience emerges: that ability to recover.

Have many great leaders failed? Churchill was a political failure from the end of the First World War until 1940, and then he was thrown out of office by the electorate in May 1945, after leading the UK to victory in World War II. George Washington was soundly defeated by the British in 1776 in a series of battles around New York City, and he lost several battles after that. Lincoln's life was a series of failures—we remember the Lincoln-Douglas debates but forget that he lost that election in 1858. (Those debates took place during the race for a US senate seat in Illinois, not the American Presidency.) In none of these examples did the leader intend to fail; each was intensely ambitious, driven to succeed. In these three examples, I believe each person's character gave him the resilience to recover and continue. But despite these inspiring examples of perseverance, we should aspire to lead *without* enduring too many character-building moments brought on by failure.

Are we too tolerant of mistakes today? One of the most annoying aspects of our digital age is toleration, even a celebration, of making mistakes. And why not? We consumers are guinea pigs who endure half-baked software programs as we help the programmers identify errors they should have corrected in the first place. Contrast this laxity with endeavors that require zero defects. While I may be amused at bad singing in a high school musical, I am a staunch supporter of zero defects in aircraft maintenance. Mistakes come in many varieties; some are recoverable, but others are irreversible, and those can add up, creating a vicious cycle that leads to failure of the entire enterprise. Effective leaders know how to distinguish between correctable and intolerable mistakes. Not every mistake is a teachable moment; some are fireable moments. A practical approach for leaders is to communicate that they are not keen on mistakes overall, but will become incandescent when they are not reported.

We should work diligently to avoid the mistakes that lead to failure, and we should require others to do the same. Failure leaves a bitter taste to which we should never grow accustomed. But in your quest for success, do not use the expression I heard from one army officer at Ft. Benning, Georgia: "The one thing I won't tolerate is mediocrisy [*sic*]."

How To Succeed At Leadership By Really Trying

With apologies to one of my favorite musicals, the Pulitzer Prize-winning *How to Succeed in Business without Really Trying*, for the vast majority of charisma-deprived mere mortals, leadership requires significant work. It is a constant set of trade-offs: being alert to followers' emotions but able to deliver a tough message when required; sharing the values but possessing greater decision-making authority; and balancing the self-interest of all participants with the organizational goals. This balancing act is most important within the zone of true relationships, the group of followers bounded by Dunbar's Number, the domain of pure (and non-scalable) leadership. As your scale of authority grows, you certainly can communicate directly with thousands of employees, but the group of subordinates with whom you will have close relationships will remain small. Although digital technology has enabled much more extensive and rapid communication, pure leadership is not expandable beyond that point of close relationships.

Because of this limitation of scale, numerous leaders must be present and able to thrive at every level within an organization, creating a cascade of capable leaders. In any endeavor of scale, the leadership role can never be centralized into one person. Even if you are at the pinnacle of the organization, you may not be (nor need to be) the absolute best leader in that organization. This is not, however, an opportunity for Leadership Lite or rent-seeking leadership. You must be a capable leader, employing all three elements, worthy of imitation. But as Jethro advised Moses, you need capable leaders at every level. Some may even be better leaders than you are, and that's perfectly OK. But the higher you climb on the organizational ladder, you had better be *very* good at managing resources at that level, and that capability must increase with each promotion. Once again, this basic truism: Management capability is scalable, while pure leadership is not.

How To Determine A Leader's Success

How do you know if you're effective as a leader? Achieving organizational goals is the obvious first measure, but go beyond that in your assessment. Go to your followers. Do former subordinates still seek your advice? Do they imitate your leadership? Do *they* attract and keep talent as well? Have they been successful as leaders or as specialists since working for you? Over time, are former followers grateful for the standards you set? Did you elicit a sustained, discretionary effort from the people you have led, and are you achieving that now?

One of the most splendid epitaphs is that of Christopher Wren, the great architect of seventeenth-century England. His epitaph in St. Paul's Cathedral, translated from Latin: "If you seek his monument, look around." To paraphrase this for leaders: "If you seek an outstanding leader, look at the followers."

The Individual And The Organization

One of the clichés I have heard in many companies over the past thirty years is, "You are responsible for your own career." While individuals clearly should maintain an interest in their careers, the organization (or more accurately, the highest leadership of the organization) should employ significant resources to develop talent and, more specifically, leaders. This should be a *shared* responsibility between the organization and the individual. Organizations have no excuse for failing to develop their leaders, and yet many organizations have no program at all, while others only muster a feeble, fad-of-the-month approach. Since effective leaders are a precious resource and are possibly becoming thinner on the ground, it is time for organizations to share the burden of leadership development with their individuals.

CHAPTER 13

How To Develop Leaders In Your Organization

How To Apply These Insights To The Essential Work Of Developing Leaders

But First, A Cautionary Tale: *How Not To Assess Leaders*

I begin with a recent story of complete failure to assess leadership.

This case study relates the saga of a Silicon Valley start-up: the company Theranos, an epic of terrible judgment. My descriptions are taken from the recent book, *Bad Blood*, and from the number of articles that have emerged to describe this fiasco.[46] Elizabeth Holmes was a Stanford University dropout who founded Theranos, a company with an extremely compelling mission: to create medical devices that could analyze blood using only a pinprick (as opposed to traditional methods, which draw more blood, more painfully, from the vein). But it didn't stop there. Theranos promised it would also conduct a myriad of blood tests from this small blood sample at a significantly lower cost than current practices. Holmes certainly had her purpose nailed down. She was extraordinarily successful at getting attention and raising impressive amounts of money for her enterprise, garnering over $800 million and creating a company market valuation of $9 billion.

---

[46] Carreyrou, John. *Bad Blood: Secrets and Lies in a Silicon Valley Startup*. New York: Knopf, 2018.

"Charismatic" was a word frequently invoked to describe her.

Through personal connections and her irresistible narrative, Holmes created a board of directors consisting of luminaries, including two former secretaries of state. Sadly, as is the case with far too many corporate boards in the United States, this board appears to me to have been largely ornamental. The board members were completely taken in by Holmes's passion for the mission of Theranos; no one, it seems, bothered to look under the hood. With an average age of eighty years for board members, perhaps that lack of oversight is understandable.

The chumminess of the board contrasted sharply with the inner workings of the company. The descriptions of working inside Theranos are harrowing: Turnover was extremely high. When anyone expressed concern that things were not working correctly, they were beaten down psychologically and threatened with legal reprisals. Holmes and her bullying second-in-command used and misused every form of power short of physical force to intimidate anyone who challenged their vision.

Despite fierce resistance from Theranos, *The Wall Street Journal* published a critical article in October 2015, and the whole Theranos edifice soon collapsed. Evidence revealed that their vaunted proprietary blood test devices did not work. In most cases, blood was drawn from a vein, not by pinprick, and it was analyzed in standard blood-analysis machines, but the results were presented as if they had been done on the company's proprietary devices. Elizabeth Holmes had garnered nearly one billion dollars in investments and nine billion in valuation based on hope, with what now appears to have been a generous helping of deception.

Doesn't a board have the responsibility to assess the leadership of the enterprise? The board of Theranos never looked beyond Holmes's narrative or mesmerizing sales pitch. In 2014, one board member effusively praised Holmes's ethics: "She has probably one of the most mature and well-honed sense of ethics...that I've ever heard articulated."[47] Oh, yes, and in 2015, a few months before Theranos was exposed as a Potemkin start-up, Elizabeth Holmes was honored with a Horatio Alger

---

[47] Ibid. pg 207. The speaker is Theranos board member James Mattis.

Award from the Horatio Alger Association of Distinguished Americans for being an "exceptional leader."[48, 49]

How To Conduct Leadership Development

The Theranos example demonstrates how famous, capable, and decent people showed remarkably poor judgment regarding leadership. To help us all avoid this mistake, I shall once again assume the persona of the Virtuous Machiavelli to give advice to organizations (or more accurately, to the *leaders* of organizations) on how to develop leaders within their organizations, under three main headings: structure, assessment, and progression.

Structure

- Make the distinction between specialists and leaders. Develop a career track for each. The role of a leader is to affect followers to achieve organizational goals. The specialist, on the other hand, possesses deep expertise and works within that realm to achieve organizational goals.

- Identify the various leadership roles within your organization, which means roles where subordinates must be led (beyond a personal assistant or a small staff supporting a specialist). Start to identify which leadership roles may involve making significant changes in performance or behavior of the group being led— those will most likely be the most demanding. Be attentive to leadership roles in which one must lead highly paid specialists— those roles will also be challenging. Remember, when leading a group of *specialists*, the leader of that group must have credibility *in that specialty*, but the leader need not be the *best*-performing specialist, and in many cases may not be.

---

[48] Calling it a Potemkin start-up refers to the expression, "Potemkin Village" as a description of a wretched village hidden by an elegant façade, and is named after one of the great fawning subordinates of all time. Grigory Potemkin was a minister (and one of the many lovers) of Catherine the Great of Russia. He famously erected facades in villages that Catherine traveled through on her way to the newly conquered Crimea, to give her a false picture of prosperity in these areas. The facades would be taken down and then re-assembled further down the route.

[49] Carreyrou, John. *Bad Blood: Secrets and Lies in a Silicon Valley Startup*. New York: Knopf, 2018, pg 208.

- Identify the members of your enterprise who express a desire to take on leadership roles; they are your first cohorts to be developed. Within this aspiring set:
  - Find the right balance of ego: the people who have a desire to be part of a greater effort and the confidence to lead, but not the need to be always at the center of the effort.
  - Verify that aspiring leaders are already capable individual contributors; they should want to build on their own experiences and expertise to become effective leaders.
- Since all organizations are hierarchies, outline the progression from the most junior to the most senior leadership positions.
- Examine all leadership positions from the standpoint of capabilities required. These will vary according to the context of each position, sometimes by a wide margin. Note the differences when going from one position to the next, and be prepared to initiate "capabilities upgrades" for leaders in new positions.
- Especially in groups with deep skills, leaders must still maintain their competence in skills they have developed over time. Alternating between an individual skills assignment and a more generalist leadership assignment may be a necessary track in those situations.
- Never be vague about any aspect of leadership responsibilities you assign:
  - Describe the objective and how success is measured.
  - Provide adequate time and resources.
  - Define the authority attached to the leadership duty.
  - Make the assignment of the leader unambiguous; avoid coleaders whenever possible.
  - This precision is not an act of charity; it is to level the leadership playing field as much as possible so that the

assessment of the key leadership elements (direction, capabilities, and character) can be as accurate as possible for each individual leader.

Assessment

- Avoid the worst mistake of assessment: confusing the leader's relationship with his or her immediate boss as the best measure of the subordinate leader's leadership ability. While managing up is certainly an important capability, it should never be the overriding criterion for leadership.

- Train all assessors of subordinate leaders to recognize and disregard:

    – Flattery, to which we are all vulnerable

    – An emotionally appealing narrative about the subordinate

    – Any halo effect, or the appeal of our own reflection in the subordinate

- Train all assessors of subordinate leaders to be skeptical of:

    – Any claim of leading without any friction

    – No mention of other team members' contributions

- The key to assessing leadership is straightforward: You will know the leader by the behavior of his or her close subordinates.

    – Direction: Can subordinates articulate the purpose of the effort? Are their personal goals (their self-interest) reinforced by the overall objectives?

    – Capabilities: Are subordinates confident in their leader's abilities in his or her job? Can they give concrete examples of when the leader directly added value to the effort?

    – Character: What values do subordinates mimic in their own behavior? Are they evasive when asked to state what values their leader espouses?

– Inspiration: Do subordinates express a determination to make things better? Can they give examples of when their group has worked together to develop a significant improvement?

– Overall: Do subordinates signify that they are giving extra effort, or do they behave as if they're doing "just enough"?

– The great exception: The leadership role in which feedback from (at least some) subordinates may be predictably negative is when the leader is tasked with making a significant change in group behavior and/or performance. Depending on the severity of the challenge, this effort can take more than one year to play out, and those subordinates reluctant to change will express resentment. For this reason, experienced leaders with a solid reputation in the organization should be selected to take on this duty whenever possible, not the new kid on the block.

– Does this mean assessment should consist *only* of surveys of subordinates? No. Although this input is a vital assessment tool, evaluators should always use their own judgment—that distinctly human ability to take in information and render a decision.

Progression

- Leadership development is a *progression*. Never give the first leadership assignment late in someone's career. For example, the general counsel should never become CEO unless he or she has worked as a leader *outside* legal roles.

- In any organization beyond two layers of authority, a progression to greater leadership responsibility should be envisioned:

– In the first leadership assignments, such as heading up a committee or team, the conditions (roles, purpose, etc.) should not be haphazard; they should be carefully defined.

– As leaders assume greater responsibility and more subordinates, the range of their role capabilities should be expanded. The leaders should be assessed on how well they adjust to demands in areas beyond their own knowledge and experience. Do these developing leaders know how to leverage other people's talents to succeed while absorbing new information themselves?

– Leaders will understandably want to retain subordinates with whom they have successfully worked before. It is in the organization's best interest, however, to staff developing leaders with different subordinates periodically, to assess how they develop new people and to see how those people respond to a new leader.

– For any organization with global operations or aspirations, assignments in foreign locations are best initiated early in the leader's career. Perhaps the most difficult challenge in global, multicultural positions is to communicate and maintain core organizational values, to achieve broad understanding and acceptance.

– Assignments to change organizational behavior, whether to reset bad habits or to improve performance drastically *without also changing out the group being led*, are a significant challenge. Organizations should select leaders for these roles carefully and give them full support. The leaders selected for this task should be experienced leaders being considered for top positions later in their careers.

• In the natural progression to more authority and responsibility, the organizational pyramid for leadership becomes steeper. This gives top leadership (who should be leading the leadership development program, not a staff specialist) a pool of candidates from which to choose:

- The table stakes for advanced promotions should be direction and capabilities: Can this leader direct and manage the resources at this level? That competence must be in place to be in the running.

- With potential candidates for a promotion who have all demonstrated their ability to direct and manage, character should be the deciding factor for the final selection. Character is fairly permanent in an individual— if it is found to be deficient, it cannot be "hoped" into existence. *Never put a person with an observed major character defect in a leadership role.*

- Character is adhering to core values through behavior. Do not confuse this with likeability, superficial style, or having a "great story" or narrative. No marker automatically guarantees the existence of character: not background, not education level, not even individual achievement. For any role, character is revealed in behavior, and for a leader, it is revealed in the behavior of followers as well.

- Throughout the developing leader's career, the quality of his or her judgment should emerge:

- Can this leader accurately and quickly detect an issue's degree of importance? Can this leader sense when a value is at stake? Can he or she recognize trends and spot potential trouble?

- Is this leader comfortable learning new things? Can he or she get the jargon down quickly and then understand the fundamental issues in areas outside of his or her own expertise?

– Does this leader attract and nurture talent, and is that talent still available to the organization, not exhausted by the leader?

– Most importantly, does this leader elicit voluntary, discretionary effort from subordinates, an effort that is given, not forcibly extracted?

As the Virtuous Machiavelli, I must now address a few of these key issues in more detail, beginning with the importance of having a deliberate program for leadership development, not a Darwinian exercise in throwing people in the deep end and selecting those who somehow keep their heads above water.

Give Swimming Lessons Before Throwing Them In The Deep End

An earlier insight states that the organization ought not blindly follow the common, error-prone linear path: that the best performer in a given task or specialty is automatically the best candidate to be a leader. On the contrary: Individual skill in a specialty is not an unerring predictor of leadership ability.

How should potential leaders be identified, beyond throwing mud on the wall and seeing what sticks? First, find the people who *want* to lead. Leadership requires confidence, so self-selection is a good first start. Seek people who want to take on the challenges, headaches, heartaches, and rewards of leading people. Identify this inclination early. For organizations, this advice implies that a dual-track career path should be mapped out, one for specialists (in many instances, the majority of members of the organization), and one for leaders.

As leaders move to higher positions, they become more generalist than specialist. Clearly, not all who desire to lead will prove capable of doing so, so the second step, after selecting aspiring leaders from the crowd, is to put them in leadership roles as soon, and as often, as possible, then constantly assessing the results.

Teams were the rage in business in the 1990s, and in a dynamic environment, using ad hoc, temporary groupings with a specific and temporary mission makes good sense. Putting an aspiring leader in charge of a team is an excellent developmental first start, so long as the leadership role is clearly defined and supported. As stated earlier, one of the more devious and destructive habits of bad leaders at the higher levels is to sow confusion among subordinates by not establishing clear authority in subordinate levels. Designate the team leader and give her or him the clear mandate. Above all, give the new leader the tools to succeed; clarity of authority is the first tool. The new leader should also have access to experienced leaders to ask questions and test ideas. The new leader should also have clear performance goals for both her- or himself and for the team. An aspiring leader's first leadership roles should also be in that person's areas of expertise because the organization should always try to help new leaders succeed. (The time to test the leader in the deep end of the pool should come later.)

The mantra, therefore, for the organizational leader developing future leaders is *create an environment for success for first-time leaders*. This effort is not an act of coddling, but a sensible move: We need to make organizational context as favorable as possible so that any leadership weaknesses in aspiring leaders can be identified clearly. Developing leaders must give direction, display required capabilities, and most importantly, demonstrate the character that connects with people being led. Creating a favorable environment for new leaders reduces the impact of external factors and creates a common baseline so that the key elements of leadership can be tested and assessed as accurately as possible.

With a robust structure for a leadership development program, the leaders of the program can then address the most difficult challenge: overcoming our natural biases, which can adversely affect an accurate assessment.

In Assessing Your Subordinate Leaders, It's Not About You

In developing leaders for the organization, it could be challenging to acknowledge that managing the boss is not the primary skill of effective leadership. Our emotions tell us that someone we like must be doing well. We all love flattery, especially from our subordinates, and the higher you ascend in the organization, the more you receive. But the higher boss must go *outside* of his or her relationships with specific subordinates when assessing the leadership abilities of those subordinates.

I had the great privilege to work for an outstanding leader, Colonel Stan Luallin, in the 1980s. As brigade and post commander of 2nd Brigade, 3rd Armored Division in Germany, his approach to assessing his subordinate leaders was to talk to officers and soldiers in the unit who were two levels *below* the officer being assessed. In this manner, he felt he was getting a reasonably accurate picture of how this officer was affecting the people he was leading. This method of walking around was one of the basic inputs he used to evaluate his subordinate leaders; he knew instinctively that something as complex as gauging his subordinates' leadership effectiveness required more than his own interactions with that subordinate leader.

Assessing Direction And Capabilities: The Danger Of Focusing Only On Performance

Performance of the group will always be a valid input because the success of the group is the most direct, unambiguous measure of a leader's effectiveness. If the group is failing in its mission, obviously the leader is failing as well. The cause-and-effect trail of failure must be traced, with internal and external factors placed under the microscope. Reviewing group performance should always be joined with a careful assessment of the leader, using the three key elements (direction, capabilities, and character). Did a weakness in any of the three elements contribute to the end result? Sometimes the leader needs to be replaced; depending on the assessment, she or he could be reassigned to a different leadership role, or the leader may be told that assuming leadership roles is not the correct course for him or her within the organization.

Because of the overriding importance of performance, the temptation may arise simply to say, "Leadership ability is *only* based on performance." But we must use great caution in invoking performance as the single criterion, especially if it is reduced to one measure. We all have amazing abilities to focus on one measure (our brains love simplicity), and we can demonstrate remarkable skill at achieving a measurable goal by any means possible. We must recall that companies formerly lauded as high performers (Enron, WorldCom, and Sunbeam, to name only a few) all showed great numbers, but they *really* excelled at fudging performance measures—deceptive efforts driven by their leaders. These failures caused great distress to employees, investors, and business partners, resulting in renewed calls for greater regulation.

I have observed the ability to "goose" performance targets in retailing. In one chain, a contest was announced with great fanfare: The team that produced the biggest sales increase in a month would win a trip to the Caribbean. Sales soared—and at the beginning of the next month, *returns* also soared. Associates had instructed their friends to come in toward the end of the month to make purchases in their department. The associates received the credit for the sales, and then their co-conspirators returned the temporarily purchased items to the store at the beginning of the next month. The net increase in sales was nearly zero, but first-month sales numbers looked *great*.

Performance is crucial, but it should never be the only criterion used to assess the leader. As much as we dislike complexity, as much as we love to simplify answers, we must look deeper into the leader, at some intangible qualities.

The Familiar Foundation: Purpose and Capabilities

For those of us who lack hereditary succession to give us leadership roles, we must establish our initial claim to lead through our ability to give direction and show capabilities for the role. These are the ante for joining the "leadership games" in organizations. I have observed that most egregious early leadership failures arise from obvious inabilities to give direction and to display the required capabilities. Giving direction means more than merely repeating the directions from above. From "Here's what we're going to do," the mantra must be transformed: "Here's what we're going to do, and *here's how your efforts fit into it*."

As leaders rise in the organization to more complex assignments, the ability to manage a wider range of resources becomes more important. At this level, *management* becomes a more significant part of the leader's capabilities. My view on this relationship runs against popular beliefs, for I believe that management and leadership are not opposing concepts at all. They are siblings, not separate members of warring tribes. Management ability is a *sine qua non* for leadership, especially at high levels of large organizations, because leaders must possess the ability to manage resources at that level. And managing at a larger scale is not merely an arithmetic multiplier. Managing successfully at a smaller scale does not mean that operating at a larger scale is the same thing, just increased on a larger scale. Differences in scale often bring different problems and call for different skills. Elevating a leader to a greater role without considering differences in capabilities required for that role creates significant risk.

Examples abound where a leader, successful at one level, finds him- or herself operating at a larger scale and fails miserably. The case of General Robert Nivelle, who assumed command of the French armies during the First World War, is such a warning. Nivelle was a successful commander at the field army level, and he became the commander of all French forces on the western front in late 1916, forces that had been fighting the Germans in the trenches for over two years. He organized a huge offensive for the spring of 1917, and using a tactical approach he had employed earlier on a much smaller scale, he declared a breakthrough would occur in forty-eight hours with casualties around 10,000. The breakthrough never occurred; the Germans had recently developed and implemented very effective defensive tactics that stopped the French attack. French casualties exceeded his prediction by a multiple of fifteen. In several areas along the front, the French army mutinied. Only the monumental failure of German intelligence to discover the mutiny prevented the Germans from capitalizing on the demoralization of the French forces. Nivelle was quickly replaced.

The warning for leadership development is to acknowledge the complexity of different roles, and not to fall into the trap of assuming that the demands of one position are similar to the demands at the next level up. You must define what success looks like for each position and be exceedingly attentive to the differences in roles as leaders advance.

The Most Elusive Element: Character

The leader's competence in direction and capabilities is directly observable. However, assessing character in any leadership development program will always be a work-in-progress because the element is frustratingly difficult to assess. Purely empirical measures are (at this point in time) impossible; big data will not provide the solution either, in my view. Assessment of character will, for the foreseeable future, require careful observation by the assessors.

Despite these limitations, character *must* be assessed from the beginning of any leadership development program. Any solid indicator of a character flaw, from bullying to petty cheating on expenses, should be taken into account and acted upon. The vast parade of executives who have ruined the reputations of their companies (or even driven their companies into the ground through failures of character) could have been greatly reduced had organizations not treated character as an afterthought, especially as these executives rose through the ranks. Long before Enron grew to be the seventh largest United States corporation in valuation and then, in turn, the largest bankruptcy in United States history at the time, its founder and CEO, Kenneth Lay, had frequently looked aside as reports were massaged in different parts of the organization. His behavior was definitely noticed within the company, and it fed a culture of deception in accounting that ultimately led to the financial ruin of many of his employees. If character had mattered in this culture, the debacle could have been avoided.[50]

Character is the element that emotionally connects the leader and the led, so an assessment of a leader's character must involve input from subordinates. Examples of questions or observations that can help reveal the impact of the leader's character are:

[50] Boswell, Susan. "The Smartest Guys in the Room: Management Lessons from Enron's Leaders." *Baltimore Post-Examiner,* December 22, 2012. https://baltimorepostexaminer.com/the-smartest-guys-in-the-room-management-lessons-from-enrons-leaders/2012/12/22. "Early on, problems at Enron emerged." See also, McLean, Bethany, and Peter Elkind. *The Smartest Guys in the Room: the Amazing Rise and Scandalous Fall of Enron.* New York, NY: Portfolio/Penguin, 2013, pg 23.

- Are followers inspired to give extra effort, or are they weary and worn out?

- Would they work for this leader again?

- How do followers treat their own followers? Is there positive imitation of their leader's behavior?

- How does the leader treat people—as stepping stones for him- or herself, or as investments in a better organization?

- Who stays, who goes? Who asks to leave? What do exit interviews reveal?

The exit interview is one of the best resources in any organization, but one that is woefully underutilized. Clearly, no interview will reveal purely impartial observations, but armed with the knowledge that the most common reason for people leaving their jobs is their immediate boss, we should look upon exit interviews as a significant opportunity to discern how people are being led. Above all, these vital interviews should be conducted by those in top leadership positions, not solely by a staff person from HR.

I have observed and practiced different ways to assess character:

- When I taught at West Point in the early 1980s, the head of the Department of History had an effective gauge of his officers' character: He observed how each officer treated the support staff.

- One business colleague related to me that one CEO, when conducting the final round for selecting a high-level executive, would take the candidate to lunch or dinner, but, unbeknownst to the candidate, the CEO had arranged for the waiter to make a dumb mistake during the meal. The CEO would observe how the candidate reacted to the situation.

- Narcissistic behavior is generally a good indicator of a weak character. People who treat their followers as mere training aids for their own advancement are invariably character-deprived.

- Perhaps the best advice I have received about judging character is this: When a choice arises between personal advantage and a core value, what choice do we make?

The overarching question about assessing a leader: Does this leader, with a combination of direction, capabilities, and character, inspire his or her followers in such a way that they function effectively and build upon his or her leadership to make the organization better? This standard should apply at every level of leadership.

The Leader At The Top

Since leaders at the highest levels, executives, must manage a wide range of resources and make critical decisions about their utilization, their ability as *managers* should rise proportionally to their increased levels of responsibility. Their skill as managers should confirm their capabilities in their job, and this enhances their standing as a leader.

But managerial competence should never be the sole criterion for assigning people to the top leadership positions in an organization. While leaders at the top may not be the *best* leaders in the organization, they should be *capable* leaders, and this must include demonstrating character. In far too many cases, this has not happened. Some top leaders have inherited their positions, and many are not up to the task. Others have had sudden, massive success vault them upward, without having a beneficial period of development. Others—the source of my consternation, described in the Preface—are superb individual performers who may not be leading anyone, or are celebrities who confuse influence with leadership. Too many people whose character is inversely proportional to their salary and status have been selected for the highest leadership positions. The only saving grace for us in the West is that centralized tyrannies are even worse in valuing character than is our society.

Why We Need Solid Leaders At The Top

The criterion for selecting leaders at the highest levels of the organization is simply this: select outstanding managers who are capable leaders. Candidates who emerge for these roles should be generalists who have clearly demonstrated effective leadership through direction, capabilities, and character, consistently eliciting discretionary effort from those they have led. This is a very high bar, but a high bar is needed to offset the perennial crises of bad leadership, promotion for the wrong reasons, which give us:

- The well-intentioned failure, who believes that some special factor alone (his or her own winning personality, his or her authority, emotional appeal, a compelling narrative) will guarantee success.

- The panderer to fleeting popularity, who sees harmony as an end in itself, possesses elastic standards and values, and shirks the authority of the role.

- Leadership Lite, the effective manager with no character, who leaves no enduring inspiration.

- The corrupt leader, the extreme form of Leadership Lite, who knows only one note—me, me, me.

- The rent-seeking leader in the Executive Bubble, whose primary skill is avoiding his or her leadership responsibility for the people being led.

Any of these bad leaders will poison the organization.

The best factor to mitigate these destructive tendencies is, from a set of competent managers, making character the deliberate factor in selecting leaders, rather than assuming character always attaches to success, position, or individual skill. To assess character requires deliberate effort, and the effort will always be imperfect. But this effort must be made, for it is an essential step in protecting us from the abuses that are always possible in any exercise of power.

Therefore, organizations have an obligation to develop leaders, not defer to a Darwinian struggle that rewards whoever remains standing. We should know the elements that identify effective leaders; we must now channel our collective actions to link these elements to leadership development.

Why We Need Leaders

If, as the current estimate tells us, modern humans have been around for 200,000 years, we have spent most of our existence being isolated, afraid, and without improvements in our miserable lives.[51] Civilization is, at most, 6,000 years old, and industrialization is only 200 years old. Today we enjoy a world of incredible progress, cumulative improvement, and abundance—but this is not guaranteed to continue. Natural or environmental disasters, epidemics, human malevolence, human stupidity, or any combination of these factors could seriously alter our present condition.

Our small groups, organizations, and societies must develop different forms of talent to continue to prosper. Leadership is one of those vital talents. The ability to affect people to achieve organizational goals is not a universal talent. It is a precious talent that must be encouraged and developed. There are, of course, other options:

- Arrange for a mechanical selection of leaders, like heredity
- Promote leaders based on how much you like them, especially on how good they make you feel about yourself
- Promote leaders based on performance alone, irrespective of how that performance is achieved
- Give the leader at the top full control over everything (the laziest and most dangerous option)

By giving the leader highest in the hierarchy complete control over everything, some progress may be made in the short run, but such dominance will ultimately only serve the individual leader's vanity and will eventually destroy cumulative improvement; then regression will follow.[52]

The truest leadership is practiced where authority is well-defined but limited, where followers have some degree of choice and autonomy, and

---

[51] Thomas Hobbes was correct. Using his words, life was indeed "solitary, poor, nasty, brutish, and short." When one looks at the scant evidence we have of life before farming, the record is grim. Whether we look at Ötzi, the Ice Man in northern Italy (5,000 years old); the Kennewick Man from Washington State (9,000 years old) or Naia, the body of a young woman found in Mexico (12,000 years old), they all showed signs of several injuries throughout their lives. Some had parasites and malnutrition. Each died at a relatively young age. Life was relentlessly difficult. Even King Tut (3,300 years ago), who was certainly no ordinary guy, suffered from malaria, an impacted tooth, and bone injuries.

[52] For spectacular evidence of how things, even now, can regress with alarming speed, see Venezuela.

where that delicate merging of individual self-interest and the needs of the group can be achieved. In that difficult-to-achieve sweet spot, the group does not exclusively serve the leader but serves the larger goals *through* the leader. Within this brilliant balance, individuals are inspired to do more than simply get by, and an ethic of constant improvement is encouraged. This has occurred rarely on a large scale in history, and for only a tiny fraction of the time of our total human existence—we cannot throw this away.

We cannot continue to confuse celebrity with leadership ability. People can achieve notoriety for many reasons, many of which have no connection to leadership. We also must grasp that status, even in large organizations, does not inevitably indicate leadership ability. Finally, although not everyone is a leader, leaders must be distributed throughout all organizations and society, because our need for relationships requires that we be led directly.

Leaders fill a distinctly human requirement. At every level of our activities, we need leaders to give direction, to devote their abilities to the effort, and to show their commitment to values, those precious markers that define what is good-in-itself. To operate at any large scale, we need a hierarchy of decision-makers who accomplish organizational goals through people. We need people to fill those roles, people who can complement their authority with the ability to influence people effectively. This is not a role for everyone. It is a role for those who desire to lead and possess the ability to lead. Leaders are essential at every level of every organization and society, and we must exert significant, focused energy to achieve that. Only this will give us the chance to continue to prosper through cumulative improvement. To develop such leaders, we need the concerted efforts of both aspiring leaders and the organizations that nurture them. These are the leaders we need, and we need them today more than ever.

About The Author

Tim Lupfer's dark secret is that he grew up in New Jersey. Once you get past the New Jersey jokes, his life has been pretty interesting. He entered West Point at the age of seventeen in 1968, and four years later he graduated first in his class. He entered an army whose culture had been severely damaged by the tumult of the recently ended Vietnam War. He served in various combat-ready units in the United States and Germany, and also attended Oxford University as a Rhodes Scholar, where he studied history. In addition, he served as an Assistant Professor at West Point, where he taught military history. In 1990 and 1991, he commanded a reinforced tank battalion (over 700 soldiers and 58 M1A1 Abrams tanks) in combat in Desert Storm.

After retiring from the army in 1992, Tim entered business. He served as an executive at R.H. Macy and Company while the company emerged from bankruptcy, and then became a management consultant. He has worked with several companies and organizations in the areas of organizational change, leadership, and ethics/compliance, including the City of New York, several financial institutions, global not-for-profits, and federal agencies. He has given numerous presentations on these topics throughout his career. He retired as a managing director from Deloitte Consulting in 2011.

Today, Tim is a writer, speaker, and independent consultant. He enjoys traveling with his wife (and high school sweetheart) of over forty-five years and trying to keep up with their seven grandchildren.

ACKNOWLEDGMENTS

First, I want to thank my writing coach, Cathy Fyock. She gave me the structure and encouragement to keep at it, and I hope this result reflects the quality of her contribution. I also want to thank all the good folks at Indie Books International for their support in publishing this book.

My entire life has been a study of leadership, from observing teachers at school and analyzing their behavior to separate the effective ones from the ineffective ones, through a military career, and finally to a business career. In the military, I was very fortunate to have served with many capable leaders, at all levels. The names are abundant, and the names I now list are representative of the best. On entering West Point, leaders like Phil Reifenberg and Tom Griffin were outstanding. The shared experiences with my classmates were irreplaceable; the insights of Atticus still guide me. I received superb teaching from Tom Griess, Si Bunting, and John Moellering. In the army, I served with inspiring superiors like Paul Baerman, Waldo Freeman, Tom Horton, and Stan Luallin, with excellent colleagues like Tom Quinn, Dale Abrahamson, Terry Moss and Don Snedeker, and with superb NCOs like John Lynch and Terry Valentine, to name just a few. To work with Stan Whittlesey in Desert Storm was an honor. I have learned much from several international friends and colleagues, like Peter Harry of the Royal Regiment of Wales.

In business I discovered that most endeavors were more atomized, with less group cohesion than in the military, but I was fortunate to have had excellent mentors like Toby Stamm and Lance Brilliantine. I observed leaders at all levels to discern common themes about leadership. In my last years in consulting I was able to explore the paradox of virtue in business: most of us feel it is essential, but we have difficulty explaining why. I was fortunate to have colleagues like Nicole Sandford and Maureen Mohlenkamp in my quest to solve the riddle of ethics and compliance. I was also able to test ideas with friends with deep experience, such as Randy Jones.

Finally, regarding the most fundamental human relationships, I have seen excellent leadership exercised in the most important human endeavor: the family. I am grateful to have observed my grandparents, parents, and brothers in their family roles as leaders. I now have great delight in watching my two children raise their own families, and I hope I have helped them along the way. Above all, I have had the great joy of seeing my life companion, my wife of forty-five years, as a superb leader both in her profession and in the family. I can only hope that my own leadership has lived up to the inspiration that so many people have given me throughout my life, and that my ideas in this book will help many others to lead successfully.

ANNOTATED BIBLIOGRAPHY

General Works On Leadership

The following are the books on the general subject of leadership that I have used throughout my career.

Bass, Bernard M. *Bass & Stogdill's Handbook of Leadership*, Third Edition. The Free Press, New York, 1990. A huge reference work that covers the history of leadership research and its many studies.

Bennis, Warren. *Managing People is Like Herding Cats*. Executive Excellence Publishing, Provo, UT, 1995. Warren Bennis wrote several books on leadership, and I found this book, a collection of his essays, particularly helpful.

Drucker, Peter F. *The Effective Executive*. HarperBusiness, New York, 1993. Peter Drucker wrote numerous books during his long career as an insightful observer of management and leadership, and I have found this concise book to be very perceptive.

Kouzes, James M. and Posner, Barry Z. *The Leadership Challenge*. Jossey-Bass, San Francisco, 1995. I consider this the best book of their series on leadership.

Lutz, Bob. *Icons and Idiots*. Penguin, New York, 2013. Bob Lutz is a pure, operations-oriented "car guy." He gives a candid look at different leaders he has observed, including Lee Iacocca. My favorite line is "...most successful leaders are mentally and emotionally askew." Page 3.

McCauley, Cynthia D. Moxley, Russ S., Van Velsor, Ellen. *The Center for Creative Leadership Handbook of Leadership Development*. Jossey-Bass, San Francisco, 1998. The CCL's research is outstanding.

Prince, Howard T., General Editor. *Leadership in Organizations*. United States Military Academy Department of Behavioral Science and Leadership. Avery Publishing Group, Garden City Park, NY, 1988. One of the many editions of the textbook used at West Point.

Posner, Barry Z. and Schmidt, Warren H. Two research reports for the American Management Association: "Managerial Values and Expectations" 1982, and "Managerial Values in Perspective" 1983. I learned of these reports from a presentation by Barry Z. Posner at the New Jersey Human Resources Planning Group on October 12, 1995. These reports describe the results of a survey of US managers and a comparison of the results with similar surveys in other countries (Western Europe and Japan). The research supports the concept of the need for the combination of competence and integrity in leaders.

Wooden, John and Jamison, Steve. *Wooden on Leadership*. McGraw-Hill, New York, 2005. Although I have found most personal accounts by successful leaders to be somewhat shallow, this book is an exception. I believe John Wooden possessed a rare moral power similar to that of General of the Army George C. Marshall.

WORKS REFERENCED

Bagehot, Walter. *The English Constitution*, 1873 (republished in 2007 by Cosimo, Inc., New York, NY).

Boswell, Susan. "The Smartest Guys in the Room: Management Lessons from Enron's Leaders." *Baltimore Post-Examiner*, December 22, 2012. https://baltimorepostexaminer.com/the-smartest-guys-in-the-room-management-lessons-from-enrons-leaders/2012/12/22.

Browning, Robert. "Andrea Del Sarto" Poetry Foundation. Accessed February 3, 2019. https://www.poetryfoundation.org/poems/43745/andrea-del-sarto.

Carlin, George. "George Carlin—Idiot and Maniac." YouTube. June 21, 2012. Accessed February 1, 2019. https://www.youtube.com/watch?v=XWPCE2tTLZQ.

Carreyrou, John. *Bad Blood: Secrets and Lies in a Silicon Valley Startup*. New York: Knopf, 2018.

Carter, Stephen L. *Civility: Manners, Morals, and the Etiquette of Democracy*. New York: HarperPerennial, 1999.

Chicago Tribune. "Editorial: Lincoln at Gettysburg, 150 Years Later." *Chicago Tribune*. September 08, 2018. Accessed February 12, 2019. https://www.chicagotribune.com/opinion/ct-xpm-2013-11-19-ct-lincoln-gettysburg-edit-1119-20131119-story.html.

Cialdini, Robert B. *Influence: the Psychology of Persuasion*. New York: Collins, 2007.

Corcoran, Cliff. "99 Cool Facts About Babe Ruth." *Sports Illustrated*, July 14, 2013. https://www.si.com/mlb/strike-zone/2013/07/12/99-cool-facts-about-babe-ruth.

Damasio, Antonio. *Descartes' Error: Emotion, Reason and the Human Brain*. New York: Avon Books, 1994.

DeAngelis, Tori. "Why We Overestimate Our Competence." American Psychological Association. *Monitor on Psychology*, February 2003. https://www.apa.org/monitor/feb03/overestimate.

"Digital Media and Society: Implications in a Hyperconnected Era." World Economic Forum. Accessed February 13, 2019. https://www.weforum.org/reports/digital-media-and-society-implications-in-a-hyperconnected-era.

Erez, Amir, Vilmos F. Misangyi, Diane E. Johnson, Marcie A. Lepine, and Kent C. Halverson. "Stirring the Hearts of Followers: Charismatic Leadership as the Transferal of Affect." *Journal of Applied Psychology* 93, no. 3 (2008): 602–16. https://doi.org/10.1037/0021-9010.93.3.602.

Foreman, Jonathan. "How Comanche Indians Butchered Babies and Roasted Enemies Alive." *Daily Mail Online*. Associated Newspapers, August 23, 2013. https://www.dailymail.co.uk/news/article-2396760/How-Comanche-Indians-butchered-babies-roasted-enemies-alive.html.

Grady, Denise. "The Vision Thing: Mainly in The Brain." *Discover* magazine, June 1, 1993. http://discovermagazine.com/1993/jun/thevisionthingma227.

Haidt, Jonathan. *The Righteous Mind: Why Good People Are Divided by Politics and Religion*. London: Pantheon, 2012.

Konnikova, Maria. "The Limits of Friendship." *The New Yorker*. The New Yorker, October 7, 2014. https://www.newyorker.com/science/maria-konnikova/social-media-affect-math-dunbar-number-friendships.

Kruger, J., and D. Dunning. "Unskilled and Unaware of It: How Difficulties in Recognizing One's Own Incompetence Lead to Inflated Self-assessments." *Current Neurology and Neuroscience*

Reports. December 1999. Accessed February 13, 2019. https://www.ncbi.nlm.nih.gov/pubmed/10626367/.

Marquet, David. "How Great Leaders Serve Others." TEDxScottAFB. YouTube. June 21, 2012. Accessed February 08, 2019. https://youtu.be/DLRH5J_93LQ.

McLean, Bethany, and Peter Elkind. *The Smartest Guys in the Room: the Amazing Rise and Scandalous Fall of Enron*. New York, NY: Portfolio/Penguin, 2013.

Miller, George A. "The Magical Number Seven, plus or Minus Two: Some Limits on Our Capacity for Processing Information." *Psychological Review* 63, no. 2 (1956): 81–97. https://doi.org/10.1037/h0043158.

Ng, David, Ryan Faughnder, and Andrea Chang. "Working for Harvey Weinstein Was a Coveted Career Steppingstone That Came at a Price." *Los Angeles Times*. October 14, 2017. https://www.latimes.com/business/hollywood/la-fi-ct-weinstein-employees-20171014-story.html.

Peter, Laurence F., and Raymond Hull. *The Peter Principle*. New York, NY: William Morrow & Co., 1969.

Piekema, Carinne. "Does Money Really Motivate People?" *BBC Future*. BBC, November 18, 2014. http://www.bbc.com/future/story/20120509-is-it-all-about-the-money.

Plutarch, John Dryden, and Arthur Hugh Clough. *Plutarch: The Lives of the Noble Grecians and Romans*. New York: Modern Library, 1992.

Riggio, Ronald F. "5 Reasons Why Money Is a Poor Work Motivator." *Psychology Today*. Sussex Publishers, May 3, 2018. https://www.psychologytoday.com/us/blog/cutting-edge-leadership/201805/5-reasons-why-money-is-poor-work-motivator.

Rodriguez, Ashley. "How Powerful Was Harvey Weinstein? Almost No One Has Been Thanked at the Oscars More." *Quartz*. October

14, 2017. https://qz.com/1101213/harvey-weinstein-is-one-of-the-most-thanked-people-in-oscars-history/.

Schein, Edgar H. *Organizational Culture and Leadership*. San Francisco, CA: Jossey-Bass.

Smith, Adam. *The Wealth of Nations*. Modern Library Edition. New York: Random House, 1937.

Smith, Douglas K. *Taking Charge of Change: 10 Principles for Managing People and Performance*. Reading, MA: Addison-Wesley Pub. Co., 1996.

Sward, Susan. "10 Days That Shook S.F." SFGate. *San Francisco Chronicle*, February 9, 2012. https://www.sfgate.com/news/article/10-days-that-shook-S-F-3184971.php.

Turkle, Sherry. *Alone Together: Why We Expect More From Technology and Less from Each Other*. New York: Basic Books, a member of the Perseus Books Group, 2012.

"Together, Technology and Teachers Can Revamp Schools." *The Economist*, July 22, 2017. https://www.economist.com/leaders/2017/07/22/together-technology-and-teachers-can-revamp-schools.

Vincent, James. "Watch Jordan Peele use AI to make Barack Obama deliver a PSA about fake news." TheVerge.com, April 17, 2018. https://www.theverge.com/tldr/2018/4/17/17247334/ai-fake-news-video-barack-obama-jordan-peele-buzzfeed

Walker, Angelina. "Nursing Satisfaction Impacts Patient Outcomes, Mortality." Nurse.org. Accessed March 12, 2019. https://nurse.org/articles/nursing-satisfaction-patient-results/.

Whitbourne, Susan Krauss. "In-Groups, Out-Groups, and the Psychology of Crowds." *Psychology Today*. Sussex Publishers, December 10, 2010. https://www.psychologytoday.com/us/blog/fulfillment-any-age/201012/in-groups-out-groups-and-the-psychology-crowds.

Yagoda, Ben. "Your Lying Mind: The Cognitive Biases Tricking Your Brain." *The Atlantic*. Atlantic Media Company, August 7, 2018. https://www.theatlantic.com/magazine/archive/2018/09/cognitive-bias/565775/.

Ziv, Stav. "At Oscars, Harvey Weinstein Thanked More than God, According to 2015 Analysis." *Newsweek*, October 10, 2017. https://www.newsweek.com/oscars-harvey-weinstein-thanked-more-god-according-2015-analysis-681593.

Made in the USA
Middletown, DE
09 January 2020